Getting a Grip on
LEADERSHIP

Getting a Grip on
LEADERSHIP

How to learn leadership without
making all the mistakes yourself!

A *practical, proven*
leadership guide

for
business owners
managers and employees
volunteer and community leaders
teachers and students
aspiring leaders

Robyn Pearce (New Zealand)
and
LaVonn Steiner (USA)

Disclaimer
Check with your legal, accounting and business advisers before implementing any advice in this book. While the best possible care has been taken in researching and presenting this material, practices vary in different countries, and from year to year. The authors and publisher take no responsibility for the operation of your business.

Published by Reed Books, a division of Reed Publishing (NZ) Ltd,
39 Rawene Road, Birkenhead, Auckland 10.
Associated companies, branches and representatives throughout the world.

This book is copyright. Except for the purposes of fair reviewing, not part of this publication may be reproduced or transmitted in any form or by any means, electronic or mechanical, including photocopying, recording, or any information storage and retrieval system, without permission in writing from the publisher.
Infringers of copyright render themselves liable to prosecution.

A catalogue record for this book is available from the National Library of New Zealand.

© 2004 Robyn Pearce and LaVonn Steiner
The authors assert their moral rights in the work.

ISBN 0 7900 0937 4
First published 2004

Project editor Carolyn Lagahetau
Edited by Brian O'Flaherty

Printed in China

contents

Introduction 7

Part One: The Foundation
who are you? to lead others, first know yourself

1 Let's get it right from the start — who are you, and what's your purpose? 12
2 What do you stand for (or not stand for)? 19
3 History is a great teacher 25
4 The place of power 33
5 Here I come, world — I'm good at this! 44
Summary of Part One 52

Part Two: The Vision and Strategy
where are you and your organisation going?
a good captain always has a plan

6 All planning is not the same — learn to think strategically 59
7 Twelve steps in strategic planning 68
8 Strategic planning for life 82
Summary of Part Two 86

Part Three: The Climate
what's it like to work here?
how to build a positive workplace

9 The individual in the workplace — each one makes a difference ... 95
10 Communication is king! ... 114
11 How the leader impacts the climate ... 133
12 Feedback, criticism and appraisals ... 159
13 How to deal with conflict ... 171
14 How to get the message not only delivered but also understood ... 184
Summary of Part Three ... 195

Part Four: The Synergy
how to work well together

15 What are my team's wants, needs and strengths? ... 206
16 How do I get the best out of them? ... 223
17 Into the future — leaders who can lead through change ... 244
Summary of Part Four ... 260

Last words ... 263
Appendices ... 264
Resources ... 270
Bibliography ... 271
About the authors ... 274
Index ... 277

introduction

If any of the following questions ring bells for you, you'll be relieved to know that in your hands right now you have a blueprint — designed to help you learn leadership without making all the mistakes yourself.

Are you your own worst critic?

Do you get caught up in power struggles or turf battles at work?

Are you a perfectionist and if you can't do it right the first time, you don't do it at all?

Do you ever feel overwhelmed or out of control?

Are you searching for more peace at work and at home?

*Have you ever heard yourself exclaim: 'But I **told** them how to do it!'(or some variation on the theme)?*

Perhaps you've had staff members grumbling into their coffee cup, or the boss jumping up and down, or worse, key clients threatening to take their business elsewhere. Your staff don't seem able to manage without your constant supervision; you're overloaded with work; your family complains that they need a photo on the fridge to remind themselves what you look like; and you're feeling increasingly frustrated with your role.

Or maybe you're running a voluntary organisation, and some of your committee have let you down. That's even harder

introduction

— you can't get too tough or you'll find yourself running the whole show! You rely on their good nature to contribute: there's no pay packet to hold over their head as an 'inducement' to perform!

Then, hard on the heels of your frustration, you begin to doubt yourself. What sort of leader are you? Should you give up and crawl under a rock? Take early retirement and disappear into the sunset? Go back to your old job and pretend you've no ambitions to succeed at a higher level?

You start to wonder: was there some way you could have explained yourself better? But how to learn? If you're like many people who find themselves in management or leadership positions, you've had minimal training for your role. You may have been very good at some part of the business, but that doesn't automatically confer leadership brilliance.

What both authors have learned through years of trial and error is the need for a practical 'how-to' guide for managers and leaders — but the shelves are pretty bare.

So how have people learned these skills?

☆ Most people learn by trial and error, making mistakes as they go.

☆ In-house mentoring from other managers is valuable but usually fragmented, relevant mostly to specific topical issues.

☆ Volumes have been written on leadership attributes, Fortune 500 CEOs and leadership theory, but little on *how* to be a leader.

☆ Leadership is taught as *knowledge* but leadership is a *competency*: a competency includes not only knowledge, but also skills and attitudes.

introduction

☆ Of the books that are practical, many of their examples are of top leaders, so far removed from the day-to-day experience of most folk that acquiring their skill seems like an impossible dream. We've used real examples of ordinary folk doing extraordinary work.

This book won't solve *all* your challenges. You will still make mistakes. But now you have an easy reference book with a step-by-step process, and real-life examples to encourage you when hidden alligators snap at your oars and threaten to tip your boat!

We haven't spent time debating semantics like the difference between leadership and management. In fact, we've chosen to use the terms interchangeably. Some pundits say management first, leadership second. Others vow the reverse. At the end of the day, does it really matter? The folk we work with just want the simple explanations; they've got jobs to do, and they just want to get on and do them to the best of their ability. The real question is: who have you inspired today?

Managers and would-be leaders crave for a system; you've now got it in your hands.

So, what's this system?

There are four essential commonsense components of leadership, four questions to answer. Apart from a few obvious shifts of emphasis, they're the same commonsense basics for individuals in their personal relationships, people running teams within commercial organisations, and those who make a contribution with some form of voluntary service.

1. **The Foundation**: who are you? To lead others, first know yourself.

introduction

2 **The Vision and Strategy**: where are you and your organisation going? A good captain always has a plan.

3 **The Climate**: what's it like to work here? How to build a positive workplace.

4 **The Synergy**: how to work well together.

Without these four fundamentals, lasting leadership will not take place. However, when they are bedded in, performance improves, profits increase, and people grow. A good leader does two things:

☆ Develops people

☆ Gets results.

Figure 1 • The 'Getting a Grip on Leadership' system

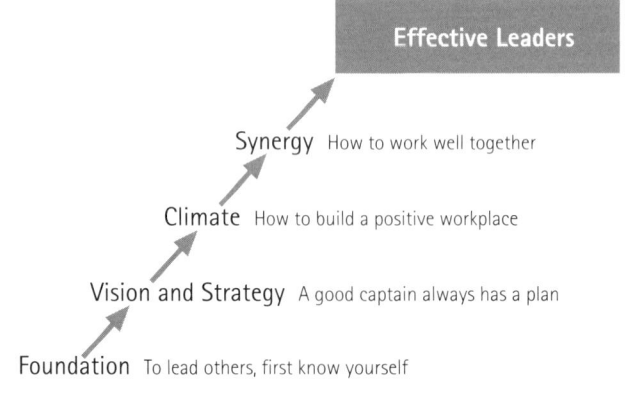

part one
the foundation
who are you? to lead others, first know yourself

1
let's get it right from the start

who are you, and what's your purpose?

In this chapter you'll consider:

☆ Yourself — the raw material

☆ Purpose — your fingerprint on the world

Like any good building, the foundation must be laid. About now you might be wondering what possibly could be the foundation blocks for leadership? Is it charisma, brilliant communication, amazing knowledge? Where do you start?

No, it begins with something even more fundamental. We don't go down to a store to buy starter materials for leadership — you're the raw material, so let's start there.

Foundation Block One:
who are you?

You might think: 'But I just want to learn to lead. Why ask "Who am I?"? Give me the practical stuff — now!'

let's get it right from the start

Just trust us on this — you'll reap the benefits soon!

The better you know yourself, the better you lead. Your foundation is formed by what you believe, what you've learned and how you live. It's your anchor in the midst of chaos. It's the centre you seek to make decisions, take action, and influence others. When your foundation is rock-solid you create unity and trust. When your foundation is fragile or incongruent you create division and distrust.

So, roll up your sleeves — you're about to do some work! You might find it valuable to start a folder in your computer for the exercises you'll work through. Or perhaps computers give you bad-hair days and you'd much rather enjoy the delights of a notebook you can carry around. Either is fine, but do yourself a favour and record your discoveries — the faintest pencil is more permanent than the sharpest mind.

In the next few chapters you'll do a series of exercises to unwrap some of life's *big* questions, questions like:

☆ What do I stand for?

☆ What lessons have I learned?

☆ Where's my power?

☆ What am I good at?

Foundation Block Two:
what is your purpose?

Your personal purpose is a single sentence that defines your core gift to the world. Each of us is responsible for using our purpose to leave the world a better place than we found it. It's your fingerprint on the world. Each of us has a unique combination

part one: the foundation

of beliefs and talents: we each have our own individual life script. It's not what we *do* in life; it's not our role or job. Our purpose is what we *bring* to our role or job. It's the big 'Why am I here?' question. Clue — to discover it, we must let go of our ego.

As you seek clarity you'll find the benefits apply not only to individuals, but also to organisations. Clarity starts from the inside: it only becomes visible to others if our actions are congruent with our mental vision of who we are.

Pat is a nurse in a large school system of 2000 students. Any nurse could fill her position as school nurse, but no one could do the job just as Pat does it.

Pat's love, acceptance and delight in children are her uniqueness. She knows she cannot heal all the abuse, fill all the needs or address all the injustices she sees. However, when she's with a child she can be totally present — a priceless gift. At work, at home, or anywhere in between, Pat lives the purpose she's identified — To be present to each child.

Because our purpose comes so naturally, we may not be able to see it easily. But someone watching Pat interact with the children she loves could help her identify her core purpose, if she didn't know it. It's what makes her unique. It's what drives her. It's the oil in the engine room of her soul, her reason to be at work.

It would be easy to be overwhelmed with the sheer volume of need in a job like Pat's. However, by staying true to her own purpose, by not trying to be all things to all people, she makes a difference to far more individuals than if she tried to spread herself too thin. And she has great job satisfaction as well.

Exercise: what is your purpose?

Aim to reduce your thoughts to a single sentence. Use the following list for thought starters.

- What am I good at?

- What do my friends say is my greatest gift? (If you're stuck and can't see it, ask a friend to help. We're often too close to recognise it.)

- Where is my power?

- What do I do because of my greatest hurt?

- What do I care about?

- Where's my passion? (Clue: when you're engaged in something you're passionate about, time passes in a flash — you're completely engrossed.)

- What brings me a strong feeling of satisfaction and joy?

- What is it I do that makes the world a better place?

Example

Wayne found it hard to identify his purpose. One of his colleagues said, 'Buddy, you bring out the best in others.' However, that didn't feel quite right to Wayne. While it was true that helping others achieve did drive him, he knew he had to dig deeper. So he asked himself *how* or *why* he 'brought out the best'. He then realised that a positive environment was equally important to him, in all areas — home, work, and community activities. *To bring out the best in the people around me, so we can all operate in a positive environment* was his final sentence.

part one: the foundation

My purpose is: ....

....

....

....

....

....

Individual purpose versus organisational mission

Purpose and mission are sometimes used interchangeably, but are not really the same. 'Purpose' answers the question '*Who are you?*' and is more commonly used for an individual. 'Mission' answers the question '*What do you do?*' and tends to be used to describe an organisation's reason for being.

An association was experiencing a shake-up. A new president had taken over, and all manner of things needing urgent attention were brought to the surface, including serious financial problems. It seemed all very overwhelming, until one of the experienced members said, 'What's our mission? If we start from there the priorities become obvious, and the course of action will also be clear.'

His advice bore fruit — they very quickly got back on track, with a clear sense of 'next steps' to follow. The challenges didn't go away, not everybody agreed on every detail, but the president had a clear path and mandate to work towards.

let's get it right from the start

> **An organisational example**
> The mission of the National Management Association of America is to provide management and leadership development opportunities and related chapter activities that meet the needs of the members and contribute to the sponsoring organisations.

Exercise: what is your organisational mission statement?

Aim to reduce your thoughts to a single sentence. Here are some starters:

- What do we do?
- Whom do we serve?
- What value do we bring?
- What are the outcomes of what we do?

My/our organisational mission statement is: ....

....

....

....

....

....

part one: the foundation

Leadership lessons

- ☑ Great leadership doesn't begin with great charisma, communication skills or knowledge. It begins with knowing yourself, and what you stand for.

- ☑ Understand your fingerprint on the world.

- ☑ Clarity starts from the inside: it only becomes visible to others if our actions are congruent with our internal mental picture of ourselves.

2
what do you stand for (or not stand for)?

In this chapter you'll consider:

☆ Values and congruence

☆ Examples of leaders who display both sides of the coin

Foundation Block Three:
values and congruence

Although values and congruence could each take up volumes, for this practical handbook let's link them, for they are very interconnected.

Values

Written values count. Spoken values count. But lived values count more. Each of us shows what we really value in two ways:

☆ How we spend our time

☆ How we spend our money

part one: the foundation

While each of us has many values, the burning question is: 'What are our core values?' *Core values* are the top four or five values we absolutely will not compromise, no matter who's looking. When we clearly know our core values, we have an anchor for decisions, choices and actions. Even as the world around us changes, our core values do not change. They anchor us. And the more congruently we live, bringing our actions into harmony with core values, the more peace we feel and the more effective we are as human beings.

Some people will say, 'My top values are: family first, health second, and work third.' However, their *lived values* are: work first, health second, and family third — with the family getting just the leftovers. Or they say they value integrity, but their business dealings show a lack of it. And as soon as we let incongruence slide in, our centre becomes rotten and we become less effective.

Congruence

When we're new in a position, it's easy to give out unclear messages to our associates. It's not surprising, since we're still learning what the role entails, and most people will be tolerant for a short while. However, if as a new manager we continue to show a lack of congruence between our actions and our words, we quickly lose the respect of our associates.

Example 1: John's story
John owned a seminar company. He was a great salesman, with a large organisation supporting him, and he ran some excellent programmes that he'd bought the rights to. He talked constantly about team, harmony, positive thinking, goal setting and taking control of your life; he also put large emphasis on family and honesty.

If he had only run short programmes the inconsistencies wouldn't

what do you stand for (or not stand for)?

have been so obvious. But he saw a cash cow. He asked himself: 'Once you've got people in the door, how can you keep them with you, spending money?' So he ran long-running seminars over a period of months, and constantly sold further programmes. It was quite common for customers to spend thousands of dollars with him.

The longer people hung around, turning up each week to his seminars, the more they picked up serious inconsistencies. His staff turnover was high; his people often looked unhappy or resentful. He preached honesty and integrity, but his clients found themselves always encouraged to spend more and more money with his company, even if he knew they were struggling financially. In the business community, whenever his name was mentioned, people were warned to keep their money well buried in their pockets.

His ex-staff, without exception, had nothing good to say about him and their financial dealings with him.

He talked about quality of life, worked crazy hours, demanded the same from his staff, and then his marriage broke up.

Those around him eventually realised that he lacked congruity: what he said and what he did simply didn't match. As soon as this realisation dawned, instead of being drawn to him, which had been the initial experience, they found themselves repelled — and wanted nothing more to do with him. It seemed that he could only hold 'followers' for a short time. His incongruence made for a very expensive business: he had to keep recruiting new staff and seeking new clients all the time. If he hadn't been such a good salesman he would have gone broke years before!

People like John are circling sharks ready to pick off unwary swimmers. However, most of us aren't dishonest: we just flounder through turbulent seas, swept by waves of increasing expectations, change and chaos. In today's fast-paced world many people haven't sat on a quiet beach long enough to get a clear

part one: the foundation

perspective of their core values — the overall guidelines that will give their swim through the waters of life a clear structure.

Example 2: Roy's story

Roy worked for a small and effective firm. It had lean budgets, slim margins and a tight focus on costs. He and his sales manager went on a sales trip together. They were each given a cash travel allocation, which turned out to be more than was needed. When they returned, the sales manager told Roy, 'Just keep the difference. They expect you to spend it.'

Roy knew that wasn't true: he'd overheard the managing director ask the sales manager to keep a lid on expenses, and to turn in any surplus. For Roy, keeping the difference was the same as stealing money from the firm, so he quietly returned it to the accounts department.

The firm's accountant mentioned it to the managing director. A few months later the sales manager was let go, and Roy was invited to take his position. There were other factors, but it also came out that the previous fellow had constantly spent to the limit of all expense accounts. Roy's quiet honesty had been noted. Having proved himself trustworthy in small things, he was given the chance to expand into higher responsibility.

We all need to constantly re-evaluate our actions through the filter of values and congruence, and none more so than a leader.

A lack of fundamental guidelines causes stress, not only to ourselves but also to those who work for us, increased stress leads to burnout, and we lose good employees or associates. One of the leader's survival skills for the future is stress-busting, the ability to spot signs of stress and burnout in themselves and others. Leaders manage energy; stress leaks it.

what do you stand for (or not stand for)?

Exercise: values

Write down your top four or five core values, and analyse your regular actions in that light. Think about where you spend your time and money and how you've lived your life. If you get stuck, the following list of values will prompt you.

Core values

1 ....
2 ....
3 ....
4 ....
5 ....

Figure 2 • Values examples

Accuracy	Creativity	Family	Play	Success
Achievement	Credibility	Freedom	Pleasure	Supportive
Adventure	Decisiveness	Fun	Quality	Teamwork
Affection	Dependability	Health	Recognition	Technology
Autonomy	Discipline	Honesty	Relationships	Time
Balance	Effectiveness	Honour	Reliability	Trust
Challenge	Efficiency	Hospitality	Respect	Uniqueness
Commitment	Enthusiasm	Innovation	Responsibility	Variety
Compassion	Entrepreneurial	Integrity	Results	Visionary
Competence	Excellence	Leadership	Safety	Wisdom
Competition	Expertness	Learning	Service	Work
Contribution	Fairness	Loyalty	Solutions	
Cooperation	Faith	Money	Status	

part one: the foundation

Leadership lessons

- ✔ Decisions based on the value of making as much money as possible are shallow and short-sighted, with limited results.

- ✔ Leaders must be congruent in all areas of their lives.

- ✔ Lived values count more than what's written or spoken.

- ✔ Hold fast to your values, even if no one is watching, or it goes against the crowd.

3

history is a great teacher

In this chapter you'll consider:

☆ What you've already learned in life

☆ What holds you back

☆ What is success?

☆ Role models and influencers

Foundation Block Four:
what have I already learned?

A little more introspection is required before we can move into new lessons. Life is the best teacher, as long as we've got our ears open, our eyes wide, and our brain engaged! You'll likely find that when you step back, take a look at your history, and answer the questions at the end of this chapter, the picture of who you are becomes clearer.

To help prompt your thinking, let's look at three of the elements you're about to consider: what holds us back; success; and role models and influencers.

part one: the foundation

What holds you back?

Julie was a mother and a manager. However, she was frustrated: she felt she lacked effectiveness. When she examined what was holding her back, three areas loomed:

- *Fear, uncertainty and doubt*
- *An underlying feeling that she wasn't good enough*
- *Perfectionism*

She realised her striving for perfection was rooted in wanting approval and control. And she saw that when she spent time on perfectionist tasks, she wasn't doing things with her family. Julie recognised how unhealthy it is to aim at something as unattainable as perfection; instead she decided to seek excellence, not perfection.

She also explored her influence on others. She knew she had a natural skill at motivating people, and they liked working with her. She also had an outstanding ability to organise and negotiate conflicts. As she focused more on her skills, her confidence and effectiveness grew.

Robert Browning said: 'My business is not to remake myself, but to make the absolute best of what God made.'

What is success?

Think about the buyer who goes to look at a house and arrives before the real estate salesperson. The buyer notices one of the window shades is up and, anxious to see inside, peeks in the window. All he can see is one room. Does that give him a balanced perspective? Could he make an effective buying decision based on that one view?

It's not possible to judge a house by looking into only one room; nor is it possible to judge success this way either. And yet, how often, especially in our materialistic Western world, is success defined by only one filter — money and possessions.

history is a great teacher

There has been a huge shake-out in some major corporations and their associates recently in a number of countries. Ethics (or lack of it) and greed underpin the whole sorry saga. What drives the desire for more gain, at any price? Is it also a hunger for success? And how can we define success?

Perhaps you, like us, have looked at people who have been very successful, and for a time have been most impressed by their external trappings of success and apparent effectiveness. But life has a delightful way of throwing light into dark corners. We all make mistakes, but some of those people we once admired have gone way beyond honest mistakes. They've

Figure 3 • Filters to define success

There are at least eight filters by which to define success, and you'll probably think of others:

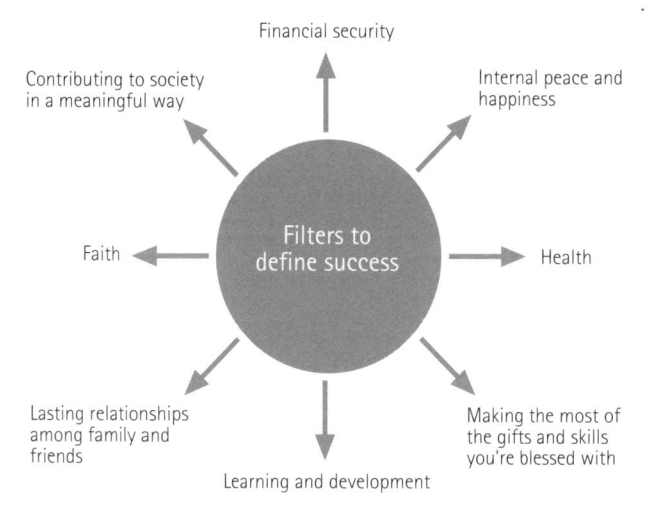

- Financial security
- Internal peace and happiness
- Health
- Making the most of the gifts and skills you're blessed with
- Learning and development
- Lasting relationships among family and friends
- Faith
- Contributing to society in a meaningful way

allowed their greed and enormous egos to sweep them, like the thundering waves of a tsunami, onto very rocky shores. Their deceit has led some of them to prison walls, to ruined lives and businesses (and adversely affected the lives of millions of innocent or naive others).

Many people now deservedly languishing in prison, or facing the distinct possibility of doing so, have defined success by what they do or have: the gaining of wealth, fame or rank. Would they be there if instead they'd had a wider definition of success, including *who* they are? I think not.

True leaders seek for ways to contribute positively to society in ways that will outlive them. They don't build their perception of success on shallow, short-term externals.

Role models and influencers

We come by business naturally in our family. Each of the seven children in our family worked in our father's store, 'Our Own Hardware-Furniture', in Mott, North Dakota. We started work with odd jobs like dusting, arranging shelves and wrapping; later we graduated to serving customers. As we worked and watched, we learned that work was about more than survival and making a sale.

It was shortly before Christmas. I was in grade seven and was working evenings, straightening the toy section. A little boy, five or six years old, came in. He was wearing a tattered brown coat with worn-out cuffs. His hair was straggly, except for a cowlick that stood straight up from the crown of his head. His shoes were scuffed and his one shoelace was torn. The little boy looked poor — too poor to afford to buy anything. I thought, 'Hmm, I bet he's going to shoplift,' and positioned myself to watch. He looked around the toy section, picked up this item and that, and carefully put them back in their place.

Dad came down the stairs and walked over to the boy. His steel blue eyes smiled and the dimple in his cheek stood out as he asked the

history is a great teacher

boy what he could do for him. The boy said he was looking for a Christmas gift to buy for his brother. I was impressed that Dad treated him with the same respect as any adult. Dad told him to take his time and look around. He did.

After about 20 minutes, the little boy carefully picked up a toy plane, walked up to my dad and asked, 'How much for this, mister?'

'How much you got?' my dad replied.

The little boy held out his hand and opened it. His hands were creased with wet lines of dirt from clutching his money. In his hand lay two dimes, a nickel, and two pennies — 27 cents. The price on the toy plane he had picked out was $3.98.

'That'll just about do it,' Dad said as he closed the sale. Dad's reply still rings in my ears. I thought about what I'd seen as I wrapped the present. When the little boy walked out of the store, I didn't notice the dirty, worn coat, the straggly hair, or the single torn shoelace. What I saw was a radiant child with a treasure.

Dad treated people right and his business flourished. His influence had a ripple effect far beyond that small community on the prairies of North Dakota.

Little did I know on that cold December night, I had just learned my greatest lesson in leadership. Respect has become my foundation principle in dealing with people. That night I learned from my dad that everyone has worth and value as a human being.

(This lesson is from one of LaVonn's role models, her dad, and was first published in *Chicken Soup for the Soul at Work*.)

part one: the foundation

Exercise: what have I learned?

Remember, often our most wonderful insights come from seemingly negative experiences, so count them too.

What have been my three most significant life lessons?

1 ....
2 ....
3 ....

What holds me back from the success or quality of life I desire?

1 ....
2 ....
3 ....

What are my top successes?

1 ....
2 ....
3 ....

How do I define success?

....
....
....
....

history is a great teacher

What have been my worst failures (as I saw them at the time)?

1 ....
2 ....
3 ....

Who are, or have been, my role models or influencers (living or dead)?

1 ....
2 ....
3 ....

How would my closest friend describe me?

1 ....
2 ....
3 ....

Who loves, or has loved me? And what can I learn from them?

....
....
....

Who has definitely *not* loved me? And what can I learn from them?

....
....
....

part one: the foundation

On the last day of my life, what must I have accomplished so I can look back on my life as having been truly satisfactory?

....
....
....
....
....
....

Leadership lessons

- Consider what lessons life has taught you.

- Every person deserves respect. They can lose it or keep it: the choice is theirs, but no one has to earn it! Human dignity requires we respect one another *regardless* of position or possessions.

- Each life is an example and an influence.

- Our unique influence grows from our life — the lessons, hurts, disappointments, joys, successes and failures we alone have experienced.

- Like a stone thrown into water, our influence has a ripple effect — often without us knowing it.

- Success is measured by a variety of factors, not just money and material wealth.

The place of power

In this chapter you'll consider:

☆ The two cardinal rules of power

☆ A 'pulse check' on your sources of power

☆ How to balance the power ledger

☆ The power of the mind

Foundation Block Five:
the two cardinal rules of power

The two cardinal rules of power are:

1　Never give away personal power.

2　Never give power to a person who *needs* it. He or she will misuse it.

A leader understands the place of power — not to be misused, but to be effective. In this very important chapter you'll examine your personal power sources. It's the juice in

part one: the foundation

your engine. It gives you strength to overcome difficulties, confidence to challenge inappropriate behaviour, and the ability to change things that are wrong. A belief that we lack power produces doubt, fear and anxiety; it holds us back from becoming the people we were meant to be. There's probably no one alive who hasn't felt powerless at some time in their lives. As children most of us learned the art of innocently giving our power away through comparison.

☆ 'My brother is smarter than I am.'

☆ 'My *sister* is the athlete in the family.'

☆ 'Jane is the organised one.'

☆ 'Steve is the favourite one.'

☆ 'I'm really not that good at maths.'

We compare our worst with someone else's best, give our power away and set ourselves up to come out on the short end. What's worse, we let others do it to us also.

Maybe you or someone you know accepted as 'truth' the negative messages you heard from others. Our mind makes mental tapes of these 'truths' and plays them over and over without us even being aware of it. We replay these negative messages long after the people who gave them to us are no longer in our life.

Negative mental tapes destroy potential. They produce doubt, fear and anxiety; they hold us back from becoming the people we were meant to be. Examples are:

☆ 'What makes you think you're good enough?'

☆ 'How could you be such a fool?'

the place of power

☆ 'I could have told you you'd fail that exam.'

☆ 'You'll never amount to anything.'

Exercise: mental tapes
What mental tapes do you play over and over in your mind? Are they positive or negative messages?

Throughout the next day carry a notebook with you. Write down quick notes regarding your thoughts. (If your work is very busy it may be easier to do this on a day off.) Identify, isolate and question negative mental tapes.

If you still find it difficult to be objective about your findings, seek an objective counsellor or someone whose judgement you trust to help analyse your findings and move you forward out of negative thought patterns.

The exercise above was life-changing for a nurse in a large acute care medical centre. Sue was nine years old when the bullying began. It started over jealousy by seven girls a grade ahead of her. It ballooned to blatant bullying with daily encounters each school day.

Through eye-rolling, taunting, mocking, Sue was demeaned, criticised and made fun of throughout adolescence. She still remembers vividly the unrelenting scorn and ridicule from these girls each time she went into the bathroom. They made fun of the way she walked, what she said, the clothes she wore and even her successes. This continued for seven years until Sue was 16 years old, and only stopped when the seven older girls graduated.

Outwardly Sue was a confident, successful young woman. She achieved in both music and academic subjects and graduated fourth in her class. Sue's friends never knew what she'd gone through; she was too embarrassed to tell anyone except her mother. As the years rolled by, an accomplished Sue was promoted to management. But like an underground stream, the invisible thought that she was an impostor flowed endlessly through her mind. Doubt, fear and anxiety about not being good enough were embedded in her head. The bullying lasted seven years; the effect of the bullying lasted 46 years.

At age 55 Sue got help. In private mentoring she questioned her mental tapes, released them and became free. She finally realised that the bullying was not about her; it was about the seven girls. Only people who feel inadequate bully others. Sue learned that if they hadn't picked her as their victim, they'd have found someone else. Today Sue's most precious gift to others is acceptance — something she'd been denied by those insecure schoolgirls.

Feeling powerless is not unusual; combating it is. Sue never once stood up to the bullies. She didn't realise she could. Further, she wouldn't have known what words to use.

Do a 'pulse check' on your sources of power

Each of us has at least six power sources we may be unaware of — power sources that are ours no matter where we are or who we're with: sources each of us can develop. And leaders, managers and parents also have position power. Leaders are responsible for engaging power sources in themselves and others.

Task power

Task power stems from doing a particular job. This is the power where we help and expedite the process or procedure or block and delay others from completing process or procedure.

Reward power

Reward power comes from our power to praise, promote, give

time off, award medals and certificates and increase pay. Conversely it includes the power to withhold rewards.

Personal power

Personal power comes from character attributes such as:

☆ vision for the future

☆ determination

☆ ability to solve problems

☆ organisation

☆ ability to communicate

These attributes are the non-tangibles we bring because of who we are. Personal power also includes our attractiveness of character or ability to satisfy the psychological needs and wants of those around us. If we have high personal power others are attracted to us and to what we can do for them.

Relationship power

Relationship power comes from the power of association with others through friendships, cultivation of network relationships, or reciprocity (someone owes us a favour).

Knowledge power

Knowledge or expert power comes from having expertise, from being able to solve problems. This is often through knowing a special skill or group of skills, but is also shown by academic degrees, or special training, continuing education or life experience. Knowledge power can often be transferred from job to job.

part one: the foundation

Spiritual power

Spiritual power comes from belief in something bigger than humanity. It's a sense of help beyond us — a power coming from an external source. You may not have an awareness of this issue but there will be many people around you who do.

Position power

Position power comes from the authority of the position we have. It's the power to manage people and resources. It's the power to influence and develop. It could include the ability to threaten, intimidate and severely punish. Parents and managers have position power.

Exercise: sources of power

If we look at these power sources as a pie graph, how large is each piece in your pie? You might also like to record the thoughts that led you to these percentages, as in the example below.

Figure 4 • Power sources pie charts

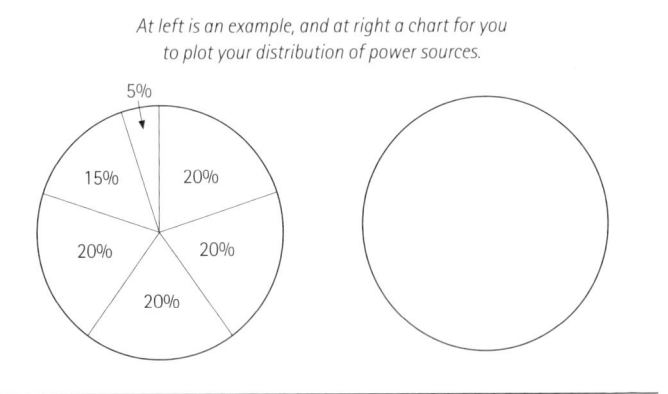

At left is an example, and at right a chart for you to plot your distribution of power sources.

5%, 15%, 20%, 20%, 20%, 20%

the place of power

EXAMPLE

20%	Personal power: the characteristics of humour, honesty, sincerity and hard work.
20%	Relationship power: the ability to easily make and retain friends, the ability to make customers laugh and feel ten feet tall.
20%	Knowledge power: I'm a well-trained, up-to-date graduate, flexible and open to learning.
20%	Spiritual power: I'm centred in faith and know I'm a good and worthwhile person.
15%	Task power: the ability to do my best at least 95 percent of the time, or not. It's my choice. How and when I do my work affects the effectiveness of the department.
5%	Reward power: not yet in a position to reward formally; I reward those around me informally at present.
0%	Position power: I am a self-leader but have no position power at the present time.

How to balance the power ledger

Generally we overestimate the power of others and underestimate our own.

Phil, a new banking employee, was at ease with customers and co-workers but was intimidated by the manager of his department. The manager was authoritative, delegating to whoever happened to be standing closest. He was often abrupt, demanding and rude — perhaps without realising it. He was more interested in results than relationships. In his presence, Phil felt powerless.

Although we are in control of our power, we can give it away without knowing it. In fact, Phil did have power. When around the manager, however, he let it slip through his fingers.

His feeling about his manager affected his sense of well-being and job satisfaction. Eventually it came to a head: change or move on. As he worked with LaVonn, he began to realise that although he found his manager rather dominant and overbearing, Phil himself was partly

part one: the foundation

responsible for the situation. By giving away power that was legitimately his, he created a power vacuum which, of course, the manager had to fill.

Imagine that every relationship you have is surrounded by an energy bubble. Nature abhors a vacuum; if one party takes up a greater part of that bubble, it forces the second person into a smaller share. Equally, if one person takes a submissive position, it forces the second into a dominant position. When a person holding a less than equal position claims his or her rightful space, the equilibrium shifts.

Figure 5 • Example of an energy bubble
with unequal power sources

Here are the six strategies Phil used to improve the situation, to balance the inequities:

☆ Be aware of what is going on

☆ Identify power sources

☆ Own your power sources

the place of power

☆ Understand your behaviour

☆ Depersonalise the situation

☆ Practise changing the equilibrium

Awareness

Name what's going on. Phil had been giving his power away unknowingly.

Power

Identify power sources. Knowledge of the seven sources of power was important to Phil. Few people know these, except on a subliminal level. Once he identified them, Phil could develop and grow them.

Ownership

Own your own power sources, no matter who you're with. Phil identified his power sources, the attitudes, skills and attributes that made him the effective employee he already was, and stopped giving undue weight to what he thought the manager 'might' be thinking.

Understanding

Recognise that dominating behaviour is a response to hidden feelings of inferiority. Phil began to realise that a person who feels secure in whom they are has no need to dominate others.

Depersonalise

Phil asked himself: 'Is this personal, or is it a common reaction that other employees have with this same manager?' It's easy to take things personally, when in many cases it's more about the other person.

part one: the foundation

Practice

He began to practise changing the equilibrium. Using the image of an energy bubble around himself and his boss, Phil pictured them as being more equal. As he armed himself mentally, his posture, energy and interaction changed.

Internal beliefs drive our behaviour. As Phil practised mental conditioning, he let his mind set the target and then subconsciously aimed at it. The image of an energy bubble with himself equal to his boss prompted a behaviour change. Phil walked taller. He stood as though he owned the ground he stood on. His voice gained assurance and he even began to suggest alternative ways of doing things.

A well-documented natural mental law says 'whatever we expect becomes our own self-fulfilling prophecy'. We never prove ourselves wrong.

Phil's new mental picture was powerful. It blocked out negative thoughts and helped him make a crucial change. As soon as he changed, his relationship with his manager changed. Think about this. If one person in a relationship changes, even if ever so slightly, it changes the balance in the relationship. This forces the other party to move, in order to stabilise — it's impossible for things to stay the same.

A point to ponder: the power of the mind

Sporting literature abounds with examples of the power of the mind; excellence in sports is said to be 90 percent mental and only 10 percent physical ability.

Phil Jackson, the legendary basketball coach who has one of the best winning percentages in NBA history, says, 'It's what's in the two top inches that counts.'

the place of power

Australian potato farmer Cliff Young was 61 when he shot from obscurity to win the tough international Sydney to Melbourne Ultra Marathon. At 75 he was still running ultra marathons and beating records. His mantra to protégée New Zealander Kim Morrison: 'It's all up here, kiddo.' At age 20 she became the youngest woman in the world to run over 100 kilometres in 24 hours. Only a short time prior to that race the longest distance she'd run was 10 kilometres!

Leadership lessons

- Never give away personal power.

- Don't give power to a person who *needs* it. He or she will misuse it.

- Bullies are inadequate and insecure people.

- You have at least six, and sometimes more, sources of power available at all times.

- We often overestimate the power of others and underestimate our own.

- Nature abhors a vacuum — if you don't claim and apply your appropriate power sources, you force others to take a disproportionate share.

- Our internal beliefs drive our behaviour.

5
here I come, world

I'm good at this!

In this chapter you'll consider:

☆ Your strengths and competencies

☆ How to link your competencies with your desires

☆ The winding path to work you really love

☆ What lights you up

Foundation Block Six:
know your strengths

To complete a solid leadership foundation, let's be very clear on what you do well.

So, what *are* you good at?

Our competencies add value to the workplace and/or any other association we're involved with, either paid or unpaid. They include technical ability, knowledge, interpersonal skills, experience, and capacity to do the job.

here I come, world

Brad, an experienced accountant, lost his job through a merger and acquisition of his company. He worried about the increased competition for accounting jobs in the area and felt anxious about his future. An out-placement adviser suggested he use this time between jobs to consider what he really wanted in life, what skills and abilities he had, what ways he'd added value in his last job.

They were great questions. Brad realised it wasn't just his skills and experience that the employer valued, but rather how he'd used them. It wasn't the flat data on the CV that mattered but, rather, the glue that bound the whole man into one well-rounded employable package. His self-leadership skills had served him well; his work history was outstanding; he brought vigour and enthusiasm to work he enjoyed.

As Brad identified his assets, his confidence grew. By connecting what he wanted with what he'd accomplished, Brad was able to set himself apart from other applicants. He won the next job he applied for.

The next exercise will help you clarify your strengths. By recording your desires, abilities and assets, you'll find it easy to see a good, clear overview of your competencies. (We've related them to work, but of course the framework for work and life are parallel — you can use it for any facet of your life.)

Exercise: know your strengths

- *Desires*: wishes; dreams; what we'd choose to do if we were certain we wouldn't fail.
- *Abilities*: skills, talents, and capacities — what we do with ease.
- *Achievements*: what we've accomplished with our abilities — the tangible value our abilities add to the workplace. Assets

part one: the foundation

are a means to set yourself apart from other applicants seeking the same position.

✒ *Competencies*: the overall picture, a composite of desires, abilities and achievements.

Figure 6 • Your competencies chart

COMPETENCIES		
DESIRES	ABILITIES	ACHIEVEMENTS

Figure 7 • Sample competencies chart

COMPETENCIES		
DESIRES	ABILITIES	ACHIEVEMENTS
To be of service to others To have autonomy To work in science To have financial security To write poetry To have lasting relationships at work and at home	Interpersonal skills Positive attitude Computer skills Organised Strong work ethic Follow-through Compassionate Good negotiator	Managed a pilot project that saved the firm $95,000. Published a newsletter Researched trends on the Internet Organised a regional conference Worked on a marketing campaign

The winding path to work you really love

Before we finish this first part of the book, let's take a look at your career choices. Did you *really* know what you wanted to be or do when you left high school, college, university (or whatever education you received)?

If you can say 'yes' you're the exception! We're asked to make very important life-shaping decisions at a time when usually we've not lived enough to know the significance of those decisions. Many people find themselves in jobs they don't like: jobs that don't inspire, excite or satisfy; jobs that quench and kill their passion and spark. How often was that path chosen because of someone else's expectation? How often were they pushed in that direction by parents, friends or hormones? Or, how often was the job perfect for them initially, but their focus has changed?

Can we do something about it? Always — but the route will vary for each person. Does it have anything to do with leadership? Absolutely — great leaders energise and inspire, and how can you do that with greatness when you're uninspired yourself?

Example 1: Mike's story

Mike's parents had an expectation that he would be a physician. His grandparents had an expectation that he would be a physician. At the time he thought, 'Why not become a physician? There's nothing else I especially want to do.' So he went to medical school.

He became very good at his job, earned excellent money, but his heart wasn't in it. Something was missing. However, the golden handcuffs were hard to shake. He didn't share his discontent with many, but one day a conversation with a close friend led down the path of 'what might have been'.

part one: the foundation

'If you could wave a magic wand and do anything you like, Mike, what would it be?'

He replied, 'I'd love to be a high school teacher. To see young minds grow and expand with new knowledge, to hear the excitement in their voices as new horizons open in front of them, to share their joy; it's one of the most rewarding things in the world for me.'

The questions he faced were:

- *Do I accept my life and career as it is, know I'm doing good work, and live with this underlying dissatisfaction?*
- *Do I follow my heart, take a risk, walk away from my huge salary and expensive but very attractive lifestyle, and become a high school teacher?*
- *Is there a middle road?*

There's no right or wrong answer, nor right or wrong time. Each of us must follow our intuition, our heart and our guidance. Today Mike is still in his same position as a physician but gets huge satisfaction from teaching medical residents in their rotation through his department. And guess what? They love being with him; for many it's the highlight of their training.

Example 2: Robyn Pearce's story

From the age of nine, I was really clear on my chosen career — I wanted to be a librarian. I loved books with a passion and just wanted to be around them. And so, of course, with that kind of clarity it wasn't hard to achieve.

Since then life has led me by a variety of convoluted paths through a number of other careers, each one perfect for a time:

- *Librarian in a small city, and then a university library (stopped when my first baby arrived).*
- *Farmer's wife and full-time mother for 11 years (six of the*

little darlings within nine years!).

- *School assistant, working in the library (a government work scheme in a country town).*
- *Tourism (loved it, but not much winter money in a summer destination).*
- *Real estate (a top seller, but wow, did I burn out from poor time-management skills! That was the kick-start that eventually took me to being a time-management specialist).*
- *Multi-level marketing (didn't achieve all my goals, but what a fabulous training ground for life).*
- *My own training and professional-speaking company (started and sold the training side three times, partly due to relocations between countries).*
- *And now — more and more writing (the dream that has simmered for over 30 years before my first book hit the streets. This book is my fifth, and there are heaps more in this fertile brain!).*

As I look back on this seemingly erratic career path, my dad's words echo. 'Nothing's wasted. Life is like a tapestry. On the front side, to the observer, there's a beautiful picture. On the back, the threads wander and weave around. It's rarely neat and tidy. One thread leads to another in a seemingly random pattern.

'When you're in the middle of it, you often feel like the threads zigzagging around the back of the tapestry. When you look back years later you can see the lovely pattern in all its colour and splendour. You look back and realise that the apparent randomness was part of God's plan for you — and it is good.'

I've learned that the skills we acquire in one arena are always transferable. I've also learned to enjoy the lessons and opportunities for growth that open up as circumstances trigger these various changes. And looking back, the same passion that pointed me at the

part one: the foundation

age of nine into the world of books is pulling me, like a strong and insistent lover, to become a full-time writer. Everything works in beautiful patterns, just like my dad said!

Exercise: what do you want?

In this exercise, let your mind wander. What answers to the following questions come from your heart? Go with your top-of-mind responses — your intuition will guide you. If you have to labour the question you're trying too hard. Move to the next question and then come back later to any 'hard' ones.

If I could do anything I wanted and was sure I could succeed, what would it be?

....

What would I really love to do?

....

What am I really good at?

....

What lights me up?

....

What activity engrosses me so much that time passes in a flash, and I hear myself say in surprise, 'Where did the time go?'

....

here I come, world

A point to ponder: a beacon in troubled times

'What lights you up' is a particularly useful laser beam question.

Andreas had a small training company. A chance came up for him to work with another consultant on a very big national training programme. Granting of the contract would dramatically change the way his company did business and require a much closer working relationship with the other consultant.

He went off with anticipation to meet the woman, but came home anxious and confused. Once serious business was on the agenda he'd seen a very different side to someone he thought he knew.

He called his mentor, who asked only one question: 'Does it light you up?'

In a flash he realised — no. It was scary, but with no corresponding thrill of excitement. It all felt heavy and hard. As he made the call to the other consultant to say 'thanks but no thanks' he felt huge rocks of worry roll quietly off his shoulders.

Leadership lessons

- ☑ It's not just what we know, and what we've achieved, but how we use that knowledge and experience that matters.
- ☑ Get clear about what you do well.
- ☑ When you love your work you inspire those around you.
- ☑ No life experience is ever wasted — everything works for good, if we look for it.
- ☑ When confused about life choices, ask yourself: 'What lights me up?'

summary of part one

Our foundation is formed by what we believe, what we've learned and how we live. It's our anchor in the midst of chaos. It's the *centre* we go to for making decisions, taking action and influencing others. When our foundation is rock-solid, we create unity and trust. When our foundation is fragile, we create division and distrust.

1 **Let's get it right from the start — who are you, and what's your purpose?**

   ☆ Great leadership doesn't begin with great charisma, communication skills or knowledge. It begins with knowing yourself, and why you are here.

   ☆ What is your fingerprint on the world?

   ☆ Clarity starts from the inside: it only becomes visible to others if our actions are congruent with our internal mental picture of ourselves.

2 **What do you stand for (or not stand for)?**

   ☆ Decisions based on the value of making as much money as possible are shallow and short-sighted, with limited results.

summary of part one

- ☆ Leaders must be congruent in all areas of their lives.
- ☆ Lived values count more than what's written or spoken.
- ☆ Hold fast to your values, even if no one's watching, or it goes against the crowd.

3 History is a great teacher

- ☆ What holds you back?
- ☆ Who were your influencers?
- ☆ Every person deserves respect. They can lose it or keep it: the choice is theirs, but no one has to earn it!
- ☆ Like a stone thrown into water, our influence has a ripple effect — often without us knowing it.
- ☆ Our unique influence grows from our life — the lessons, hurts, disappointments, joys and successes we alone have experienced.
- ☆ True success is measured by a variety of factors, not just money and material wealth.

4 The place of power

- ☆ Never give away personal power.
- ☆ Don't give power to a person who *needs* it. He or she will misuse it.
- ☆ Bullies are inadequate and insecure people.
- ☆ You have at least six, and sometimes more, sources of power available at all times.

part one: the foundation

☆ We often overestimate the power of others and underestimate our own.

☆ Nature abhors a vacuum — if you don't claim and apply your appropriate power sources, you force others to take a disproportionate share.

☆ Our internal beliefs drive our behaviour.

5   Here I come, world — I'm good at this!

☆ It's not just what we know, and what we've achieved, but how we use that knowledge and experience that matters.

☆ Get clear about what you do well.

☆ When you love your work you inspire those around you.

☆ No life experience is ever wasted — everything works for good, if we look for it.

☆ When confused about life choices, ask yourself: 'What lights me up?'

part two
the vision and strategy

where are you and your organisation going?
a good captain always has a plan

Leadership begins with self-knowledge and works its way out

We've completed one of the four components in the leadership system — foundation. We've answered one question: 'Who are you?' The question now is: 'Where are you going?'

Once we're clear on our purpose, values, strengths, weaknesses, power sources and competencies we're ready for the next step in the leadership system: planning that covers both vision and strategy.

If you've already done a lot of work on strategic planning, feel free to skip this section. However, if you'd like to 'check the pulse', especially on your strategic planning methods, you'll find here a simple outline. And if in the past you've tended to skim the surface of this very important topic, you'll certainly get great value from the next three chapters. Be warned, though: don't bother to continue unless you're prepared to *do* the process, otherwise you can't experience the benefits and will probably just waste your time! (As with a roller-coaster ride, it's all very well to *talk* about it, but experience is the only way to *know* what it's like.)

Still with us? Great. Now you've got your building blocks in place, the next step in *Getting a Grip on Leadership* is to be clear on where you need to go. If you as a leader don't have that clarity, you can be sure your team is up to their chins in swamp water, fighting off alligators of confusion with a teaspoon.

part two: the vision and strategy

Henri stepped into the position as CEO of a rural hospital. His vision was to be the benchmark rural hospital for his region. He knew his target, communicated this vision, and engaged staff in strategic planning. His hospital revamped procedures and policies, implemented a physician-friendly environment, focused on patient care, and communicated to the public the things they did really well. Staff pride is now apparent to anyone entering their facility. They attract and retain staff and physicians, have a waiting list of applicants, enjoy the confidence and trust of their community, and have an enviable reputation throughout the region. The CEO and staff, through focusing on a common vision, have realised their goals — they are indeed now the benchmark in rural hospitals.

There are three types of big-picture planning:

☆ Strategic planning — anywhere from three to 20 years

☆ Long-range planning — one to three years

☆ Short-range planning — less than one year

When they're linked they work: if you do one without the others you'll be a bit like a computer hard drive with no screen or keyboard. In the next three chapters we'll give you 12 very simple steps to effective and easy strategic planning.

Some people get scared of planning; they seem to think once it's down on paper they're committed to it, no matter what. Wrong. A plan is just a guide; of course there'll be adjustments, but if we don't start with clarity we've got a very high chance of ending up with only average results. Planning invents our future — and it's fun, exciting and energising, once you get into it. The hardest part is thinking about it and setting time aside.

Good planning takes us from where we are to where we want to be, and that's easy if our focus is clear. Yes, there'll be

part two: the vision and strategy

diversions, but they're relatively easy to incorporate and manage in appropriate ways if we're clear about our destination.

Tim, president of a healthcare alliance and a keen hunter, explained it this way.

'Hunters know where they want to go and what they want to accomplish. Once they've decided on a time and a destination, all their actions are focused on that target — they prepare their gear, check their maps, rise early on the day, take plenty of food and drink, ammunition, petrol. They drive there, they hunt, and it's pretty clear when they're successful — they either eat or carry home any results! There are times when they're led in unusual directions by their quarry, but the goal is clear, and so are the outcomes.'

Like a hunter, we need to be clear on our destination, what we want to accomplish and how we will measure results. However, hunters are effective only if they've also learned the skills relevant to their sport: they invest years into preparation, skills, practice and education — all strategic aspects that give them at least a sporting chance to enjoy a successful hunting expedition.

The next three chapters focus on the area most people find a challenge, that of strategic planning. There are plenty of good books (including Robyn's *Getting a Grip on Time*) and diary management systems that describe long- and short-range planning.

6

all planning is not the same

learn to think strategically

In this chapter you'll consider:

☆ Traditional planning

☆ The value of strategic planning

☆ How to future focus

☆ The key elements of strategic planning

☆ Strategic planning definitions

☆ There's strategic planning, and *strategic* planning!

The old way

Traditional planning is similar to driving our car by looking through the rear-view mirror — it's *reactive*. Many busy managers simply repeat one year of planning year after year.

part two: the vision and strategy

Sam seemed to always be in overload; he was a busy manager, with new staff and deadlines looming.

'Sam, I want your budget for the year.' His CEO was on the phone.

Sam's traditional response was: 'Just what I don't need! Where does she think I'm going to find two days to work on d... budgets! I'm way too busy. I'll look at the past year's figures, add a 10 percent inflation factor and jazam, that'll keep everyone quiet!'

How often have you observed not only the budgets, but also last year's services and programmes offered again? And it's very rare for goals to be written, or if they are, they're frequently treated like the budget described above. For the many organisations who use traditional planning methods it is crisis and obvious problems, rather than a forward focus, that drives change.

The value of strategic planning

Strategic planning, on the other hand, is like defensive driving. Good defensive drivers constantly scan the rear-view mirror and what's on both sides, as well as what's ahead. They're *proactive*, ready to anticipate any circumstances, prepared for any eventuality.

In Part One we stressed how leadership needs a solid foundation. The next step, strategic planning, is just as important. Each component in strategic planning will help you map your strategy for at least the next five years. (Just to stretch your thinking, many Asian companies plan for several hundred years, but we'll make it easy for you — let's stick to five years for this discussion!)

all planning is not the same

George had just been appointed to a senior administrative position in an engineering firm. As he dug below the surface of what was required, he became rather worried.

'What did I say yes to?' he asked himself. 'I don't have the knowledge or experience for this job.'

It was true. George had inherited a mess. The previous manager had been very bad at forward planning; his focus was barely a year ahead. Files were disorganised; the reputation of the department was very shaky; employees were anxious, distracted and unfocused.

And then it got worse. New safety regulation deadlines placed George on the firing line in unexplored territory. When he was hired his instructions were: 'Sort this out or we'll have to close the department.' That meant 239 people would lose jobs: he was determined not to let this happen.

'Determination and innovation got me this job. I'm going to move us forward,' he vowed to himself. 'We will be the model department for the whole firm.' His vision of a possible future excited and challenged him.

With deadlines looming, George realised planning now would save time later. He pulled together a planning team comprising supervisors, customers, employees and a top manager. Within less than one month the department mission, vision and values were identified and the planning team was busy analysing potential areas for improvement. Soon, strategic goals were identified and implementation teams selected. The planning team drew on all their reserves of enthusiasm and innovation. With clarity and commitment they computerised files and finances, communicated goals and agreed on timelines. They also planned early 'quick-hit successes' so they could build on something positive.

Employees watched. Hope rose. Focus replaced fear.

Together they turned the department around. Determined to anticipate future change, they instituted trend-watcher teams to

part two: the vision and strategy

continuously monitor industry changes. They set up a training and development plan and put new emphasis on learning. Within 14 months, by using the processes you're about to learn, the close-to-closing department became the model department for the whole firm.

How to future focus

George knew his vision, his target. He had imagined himself in a hot-air balloon looking down at the department five years into the future. He could see the model department in detail. Once he communicated this picture and engaged the team, the vision came true. Vision either may be set by the person in charge or could flow from the strategic plan.

In strategic planning it's the key goals and clear focus that drive change. Many managers know that what they do today creates the future. They understand they need a solid, well-thought-out plan to guide them as to where to put their energy. But they have no experience and no blueprint on *how* to future focus effectively. For many, the whole thing seems a bit hit-and-miss: there's a bit of science, but a lot more guesswork. If you're in that category, here come the answers.

Let's break it down to the simplest possible components. If you're like most leaders or trainee leaders, you're too busy for time-stealing complex methods. You just want the guts of it!

We can't take all the work away, but when you break it down, there are just three things to remember:

☆ Know where you are

☆ Know where you want to go

☆ Know how you'll get there

all planning is not the same

Figure 8 • Questions answered by strategic planning

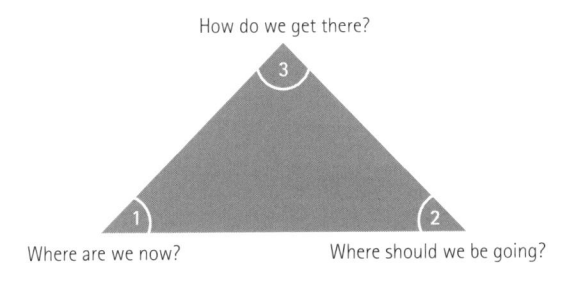

How do we get there? (3)

Where are we now? (1)   Where should we be going? (2)

The key elements of strategic planning

In the next chapters we'll dig more specifically into most of the following questions, but to get your thinking juices working, here is a list of some key elements of strategic planning. You'll see that it's a combination of big-picture thinking and analytical thinking.

You will:

☆ Examine your organisation's history for successes and failures.

☆ Analyse your organisation's mission, vision and values.

☆ Assess where you are.

☆ Ask yourself where you want to be five years from now.

☆ Ask what needs to change in order for you to achieve those goals.

☆ Explore what changes can you expect in the next five years.

☆ Discuss to what extent you, or your organisation, should be involved in these changes.

☆ Plan forward — where you need, or want, to go.

☆ Gather information.

☆ Make decisions based on opportunities, threats, strengths and weaknesses — for example, what outside trends may affect you in the future.

☆ Ask what creative and different ways there are to think about your situation.

☆ Check whether you are following old models, and if there is a better way.

Strategic planning definitions

Before you dig into these questions, strategic planning terms sometimes cause confusion, so here are some basic definitions.

Mission: why we exist

Vision: our aim; what we will be in the future; how we will look to others

Values: beliefs, ethics, standards

Scanning: a step back to take a wide-angle check, or analysis, on the environment

SWOT analysis: an acronym for strengths, weaknesses, opportunities, threats

PESTS analysis: an acronym for the gathering of data from political, economic, social/demographic, technology and specific industry environments

Critical issues: most urgent, most important issues facing the organisation in the future

Strategic goals: our 'big picture' goals

Objectives: how we will accomplish the goals

Measures: numerical target of progress (for example percentage of money saved from each transaction, percentage of population served, percentage of students achieving a specified skill level)

Evaluation: a method to determine if we're on track and on time, and what we've accomplished

There's strategic planning, and **strategic** planning!

Just as all planning is not the same, so all strategic planning is not the same. The difference is in thoroughness and objectivity. If we simply gather a team together and brainstorm what we think will challenge us in the future, the outcomes may not be valid — it's easy to get stuck in old thinking, instead of looking outside the square.

How can we avoid this? The answer is stunningly simple. Engage a facilitator to expedite the planning and outcomes. A good facilitator, as he or she follows the guidelines of strategic planning, engages every mind in the process, builds teamwork, distils ideas and documents the plan.

The facilitator

It's best to get a professional outside facilitator to guide this process. Outside facilitators keep the process on track and on time, intercept interference from egos or turf control, and make sure you accomplish the outcomes for each planning segment. Another major benefit of using an outside professional is that the managers, leaders and employees are freed up to participate in the planning process.

A facilitator brings the process, and is the catalyst: the planning team builds the plan, and it belongs to them.

The planning team

In choosing the planning team, two things are important:

☆ The number on the team

☆ The make-up of the team

Ten to 15 people is the ideal size for a planning team. This number is manageable for the facilitator, allows for diversity of ideas and experience, and makes sure you've got a reasonably sized group, even if some planning members can't attend the planning retreat.

The ideal planning team includes a combination of thinking styles: analytical, innovative, people-oriented and results-oriented thinkers. The team must include representatives from different departments or groups within your organisation and a healthy mix of big-picture and detail thinkers. It's easier to choose the people you enjoy working with, the ones who have a similar viewpoint to yourself, but by doing so you'll miss fresh and different thinking.

It's important to engage every mind in planning an organisation's future, whether they're part of the planning retreat or not: the higher the involvement, the higher the ownership and willingness to implement the plan.

Charles Darwin said, 'It is not the strongest of the species that survive, nor the most intelligent, but the one most

all planning is not the same

responsive to change.' The old system of planning, where top leaders plan and then push directives downward, doesn't work in fast times.

Roll your sleeves up, and let's get started on the 'how-to' of strategic planning.

Leadership lessons

- ☑ Traditional planning is reactive and backward-focused.
- ☑ Strategic planning is proactive and future-focused.
- ☑ Good planning by a committed team can turn around ailing departments — the key goals and clear focus drive change.
- ☑ Effective strategic planning answers three questions: Where are we now? Where should we be going? How do we get there?
- ☑ Use a good facilitator and pick a mixed team of different thinkers.
- ☑ Engage as many members of the organisation as possible: the higher the involvement, the higher the ownership.

7
twelve steps in strategic planning

In this chapter you'll consider:

☆ Pre-planning

☆ Where are we now?

☆ Where should we be going? — big-picture and analytical thinking

☆ How will we get there?

You'll find some of these steps quick to handle; others will repay a serious commitment of time. Only you know how much time to allocate. It depends on factors such as how prepared you are, what processes you've done before in this organisation, the experience of the team, how well the people work together, and how much depth you need, in order to achieve your goals.

You'll find worksheets at the end of the book in appendices 1–3a (pages 264–69), in case you'd like an outline to help with the process.

twelve steps in strategic planning

Figure 9 • Blueprint for strategic planning

Strategic Plan

Step 1: Pre-planning

- Choose the facilitator
- Set timeline and logistics
- Decide on the planning team

Steps 2–5: Where are we now?

- Review mission
- Review vision
- Review values
- Examine previous strategic plan and existing goals

Steps 6–8: Where should we be going? Our big picture

- Carry out a SWOT analysis
  - Scan externally for Opportunities & Threats
  - Scan internally for Strengths & Weaknesses
- Identify the top few critical issues

Steps 9–11: How will we get there?

- Determine goals in key goal areas
- Generate objectives, action plan and timelines
- Agree on measures

Step 12: Review and evaluate

part two: the vision and strategy

Step 1: Pre-planning

As a vision-strategic planning facilitator for over 20 years, LaVonn cautions that choosing the facilitator is crucial to the success of the process. You may find it helpful to check the facilitator is competent in each of the following:

☆ research

☆ time use

☆ tracking and evaluation methods

☆ ability to engage the team

☆ documentation

Develop a planning timeline and determine the involvement of customers, stakeholders and others in the process. Select the planning team and the location (going off-site is preferable). Once the facilitator is chosen, he or she will do most of this first step.

Steps 2 to 5: Where are we now?

Step 2: Review mission statement

Review mission statement, or identify one if not yet in existence. Why do we exist? What service do we provide? Who are our customers? A mission statement is one sentence — it may be long or short. LaVonn says, 'Often attendees don't know the mission because it's three pages long.' (Consider including the mission statement on promotional materials.)

Step 3: Review vision

Review the vision, or identify one if not yet in existence. What is our aim? What will we be in the future? How will we look to others? The vision may be identified either before or at the end of the planning. A good vision statement is also one sentence.

A simple question to find clarity — each planning member can ask, 'What do I want the organisation to look like when I leave this position?'

Step 4: Review values

Review values, or identify them if not yet in existence. What do we stand for? What are our beliefs, ethics and standards? Select the top four or five values embraced by the organisation. (Consider including the core values on promotional materials.)

Step 5: Review previous strategic plan and current goals

Review your previous strategic plan and current goals. What can we learn from what we've already done, from our past successes and failures? Are our current goals still relevant?

Steps 6 to 8: Big-picture and analytical thinking

Step 6: SWOT analysis — external scanning

In this step you run a formal external scanning — outside your organisation. Ever stood in a queue behind someone else and then found that that person is not part of the queue? And don't we feel slightly silly! Most users of the SWOT analysis process copy everyone else, and therefore don't get the results they should.

They start at the beginning, with S — Strengths and W — Weaknesses, because it's 'always done this way', they're the first

part two: the vision and strategy

two letters of the acronym (so surely that's logical), and if truth be told, it's easier to work on the things under our nose.

However, are we going to spend time on a process because it's easy, or because we want results? Here's the kicker: if you start with the back end, the O — Opportunities and T — Threats, it's much easier for your team to appreciate they have to change. It also shifts the collective thinking to a higher and more strategic perspective.

You may also like to include the acronym PESTS as a simple tool to stimulate your thinking — political, economic, social/demographic, technology and specific industry environments.

Search for trends affecting your future, but don't be bogged down by too much information. As you look at the data, narrow it down to your top five opportunities and threats.

Questions to help with your external analysis are:

☆ What trends outside your industry may affect you in the next five years?

☆ How?

☆ What is likely to change inside your industry over that time?

☆ How will your competitors change?

☆ What programmes, products or services will customers need in the future?

☆ How could you better deliver them?

☆ How will customers change?

☆ What other critical issues will impact our organisation?

twelve steps in strategic planning

Figure 10 • SWOT analysis — external scanning

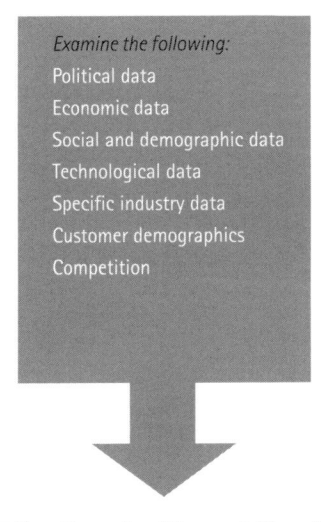

Examine the following:
Political data
Economic data
Social and demographic data
Technological data
Specific industry data
Customer demographics
Competition

5 Top Opportunities and Threats

1. ....
   ....

2. ....
   ....

3. ....
   ....

4. ....
   ....

5. ....
   ....

part two: the vision and strategy

Step 7: SWOT analysis — internal scanning

This is a formal review of your current activity, internal processes, operations — in fact, everything about your organisation.

Review current challenges, processes, standards, regulations, key factors you see that will help or impede the implementation of a new plan. This is the time to gather customer and stakeholder feedback. Then distil the five top strengths and weaknesses.

Questions to help with your internal analysis are:

- ☆ What are you presently doing that you could discontinue?
- ☆ What are you presently doing well?
- ☆ How do you know?
- ☆ How could you do things faster, easier and better?
- ☆ How will financial resources change?
- ☆ How can you best use technology?
- ☆ How will your workforce change?
- ☆ How high is the level of morale?
- ☆ Are employees working well together?
- ☆ Have you got the right people in the right positions?

twelve steps in strategic planning

Figure 11 • SWOT analysis — internal scanning

Examine the following:
Mission, Vision, Values
Previous strategic plan
Culture and management data
Financial data
Internal processes
Morale and teamwork
Services and products
Communication
Potential improvements
Customer feedback
Stakeholder feedback

5 Top Strengths and Weaknesses

1 ....
....

2 ....
....

3 ....
....

4 ....
....

5 ....
....

Step 8: Critical issues — the top few

As a fire-spotter from a high mountaintop spots danger, so scanning helps us with a bird's-eye view of a potential future. In a very powerful way, the scanning process funnels critical information we'd otherwise miss.

In the previous two steps you've identified your top strengths, weaknesses, opportunities and threats, thus completing your SWOT analysis. From that analysis now identify the top four or five critical issues. (Again, too many matters to focus on will just confuse. Keep it simple.)

If you're still struggling to find those critical issues, take a five-year perspective and consider your top strengths, weaknesses, opportunities and threats. What issues affect your ability to carry out your mission? What must you do to be where the customer will be, before they get there? How will you retain a larger pool of customers, if your market shrinks? If you change nothing, where will you be in five years?

Steps 9 to 11: How will we get there?

Step 9: Determine your goals — in key goal areas

Too many organisations have more goals than they can handle and, as a result of feeling overwhelmed, nothing gets done. Key strategic goal areas flow from critical issues, and it's only the strategic goals we need to work on here.

Key goal areas become very obvious once you've identified your critical issues; try to keep them to four or five. They define where your organisation needs to focus energy over the next five years. Caution: In this step, don't go into detail of how you'll achieve the goals. Instead, you're only defining *what* the organisation will focus on.

Once you've identified your key goal areas, don't forget to stay strategic in how they can be achieved. There may be simple ways to speed up some of the processes.

A small independent professional association was struggling with limited resources to create good systems, excellent training, brilliant programmes and an excited and growing membership. (Isn't that what all associations want!) But everything cost money and time. At times it seemed to their harried president that the task was too big and far out of reach.

Over a drink at an industry conference with the leaders of a neighbouring and much bigger association the president aired this challenge. The others looked at their colleague and said in some surprise, 'Well, why don't you link in with our administrative processes, our web-based administrative back end, our database management facility, and training programmes? The work's been done: it won't cost us anything extra (or not much) to help you.'

In one simple conversation hundreds of future hours of unnecessary voluntary labour, spread over years, were kissed gladly goodbye!

Step 10: Generate objectives, action plans and timelines

Objectives, action plans and timelines define *how* and *when* the goals will be met. We could break them out into separate steps, but let's keep it simple. Record the specific measurable steps and deadlines you'll need to reach your goals.

At the end of the strategic-planning process, the facilitator will write up your strategic plan. (Don't delegate to a junior clerical worker — a good facilitator will have expertise, objectivity and in-depth understanding of the issues.) Many organisations have huge planning manuals. If truth be known, however, managers get busy and big manuals gather dust; the

part two: the vision and strategy

danger is that these grand plans and goals, elicited at considerable time and expense, are never implemented.

> *Sarah, vice-president of sales in a multimillion-dollar environmental services company, was expressing concern about her company's strategic processes. 'We've done strategic planning but get bogged down and don't implement it. This wonderful plan arrives on my desk, and there it sits. All it does is cause me guilt and worry!'*
>
> *Her experience highlights one of the major pitfalls of strategic planning — lack of follow-through. Sarah's two previous strategic plans lacked timelines, measures and assigned accountability.*
>
> *In strategic planning we use big-picture thinking to identify the key goals and analytical thinking to identify timelines, measures and accountability. People are time-poor, but, as LaVonn explained to Sarah, if each person takes on part of the implementation, the process is simple. Once she and her team started using our process, she was elated with the results. Not only did the planning team set clear goals, agreed on by everyone, but she even earned a bonus.*
>
> *Morale soared as employees gave input. Teamwork soared as employees and board members focused on a common goal. Momentum soared as timelines and accountability resulted in rapid progress. You could feel the energy: the company was transformed.*

The guts of your future action will be decided in this Step 10, so to avoid your potential dust-gathering problem we've got two really simple and useful charts for you — the Gantt chart for timelines and the short five-column action plan that breaks actions down into simple columns. (See appendices 2–3a, pages 266–69.) You usually don't have time to fill them in during your planning time, so set a follow-up date to plan tactical steps. Either way, you need to reference them during your session to ensure necessary decisions are agreed to.

The Gantt chart is named after Henry Gantt, a pioneer in the early days of scientific management, who's remembered for his visual display to track progress and time.

With it, decide on quick outcomes you want to monitor and track in the next six to 12 months. Use it (or something similar if you've got another favourite tool) to plot your goals, objectives and projected timeline. A chart like this is a very simple visual tracking and effective communication tool.

Another way of looking at the integration of time and goals
We need to remember that timelines, although they're a useful tool, don't stand in isolation. To be effective, everything must relate to, and be integrated with, strategic goals.

Just doing this strategic planning process is a very powerful team builder: however, there's a very real danger that it might not go any further, unless several other elements are part of the recipe.

Figure 12 • Link goals and timeframes

Short-term actions 0–12 months
↓
Long-term actions 1–3 years
↓
Strategic actions 3–5 years

part two: the vision and strategy

Keys to success
The strategic goals must be driven from the top, throughout the organisation, by the CEO and the managers. When a regular check is kept on the processes agreed, it becomes an implementation plan. Get a good external facilitator/business coach. They help the management drive and monitor the implementation and agreed deadlines. Internal staff get busy with normal work; an external person keeps everyone honest and makes sure that progress is made.

Another useful tip
When our businesses were new, just like all new businesses, we found ourselves snowed under with things to do. We worked on our strategic plans by choosing just one or two themes per year (our most important goal areas). This way we made strategic progress and had a life at the same time. Try it — it may work for you.

Step 11: Agree on measures
What indicators or numerical measures will show how you're tracking to your target, or indicate your progress? For instance, it could be money, percentages, volume. Set appropriate diary dates to monitor them.

Step 12: Evaluation
This is a final review, or evaluation, of the planning process. As you wrap up your session, ask yourselves these questions:

☆ Is your plan written?

☆ Do the objectives include both a date and the person(s) responsible?

twelve steps in strategic planning

- ☆ Have you identified a timeline for objectives and action plans?
- ☆ What indicators will you use to measure progress?
- ☆ Who will monitor the plan?
- ☆ How often?
- ☆ How will you track progress?
- ☆ How will you reward progress?

Also, remember that evaluation never stops. Your good-looking strategic plan is only a guide. Sometimes you'll need to reshape it as you go.

Leadership lessons

- ☑ Break your 12 strategic planning steps into chunks and they won't overwhelm you.
- ☑ Keep the wide view — simple solutions may be waiting in the wings.
- ☑ Follow-through and follow-up are the keys to success — a strategic plan is not an expensive dust collector!
- ☑ The process must be driven from the top.
- ☑ Target the most important issues first — don't try to fix everything at once.
- ☑ Evaluation never stops.

8
strategic planning for life

In this chapter you'll consider:

☆ What you want for your life, in all areas

You probably digested the previous two chapters with your work hat on. But here's another thought: what impact do you suppose it would have on you if you did something similar for your personal life?

Many of us live life as if we have another 90 years. But life is short and limited, too important to leave to chance!

LaVonn's story
Mother had a stroke just a few years ago. She was ash white as my sister called 911. Following her stroke Mom slept for two hours. When she awoke, she sat up and looked out the window wondering whether this was to be the end of her life. As she sat there thinking, she spoke these two sentences: 'I've lived a good life. I have no regrets.'

I wonder how many people could say these two sentences? I realised I couldn't! Mom's words had a huge impact on me. They inspired me to act on a dream to take a trip to New Zealand. Would strategic planning for life

you believe that just two weeks after deciding to travel to New Zealand I opened an email requesting proposals to speak at the National Speakers Association Convention in Auckland, New Zealand? I submitted; it was accepted.

Not only did my husband and I travel to New Zealand, but I was a keynote speaker for the conference, where I met many wonderful new friends including my co-author Robyn. During our travels there, my heart nearly burst with appreciation for the beauty of the land and the people.

And I've made other changes in my life. I've laser-focused my core gift of coaching and mentoring into one-to-one executive/manager coaching. My dream is 'EXCEL leaders building EXCEL leaders on six continents.' I'm living my dreams (not just talking about them) so when I get to the end of my years, I'll be able to say as Mom did: 'I've lived a good life. I have no regrets.'

Robyn's story

A few months before I wrote these lines I received a call from my favourite aunt.

'My best friend Jean, and you know how I rely on her, has just suffered a massive stroke. They don't think she'll last the day.'

And she didn't.

By nightfall Jean, a fit and healthy woman of 70, was dead. Peggy, eight years older, was devastated — it was so unexpected.

The unexpected and overwhelming emotion for me (I didn't know Jean very well) was 'I've got to hurry.'

To be a full-time writer is my dream. Jean's passing stopped me in my tracks — was the business I'd created taking me in the direction of my greatest dreams? Could I say, like LaVonn's mother, that I had no regrets? In many areas of my life it would be a Yes, but in this one? No.

Like a flash, I realised that if I continued doing business as I was, no matter how effective and financially rewarding, writing was only

part two: the vision and strategy

ever going to be a small part of my life. Day-to-day business and making money in the 'now' were always taking precedence in my work life.

Since then I've reconstructed my business, found a writing retreat, begun to reorganise my life to create more consistent writing time — and it feels wonderful, exciting and fulfilling.

Life planning

What do *you* want in your future? If you're not sure, try the following questions. Don't analyse; instead, go with your top-of-mind responses. Your intuition will guide you to the right answers for you at this time. (And maybe the same questions in years to come will deliver different answers, which are right for that time.)

- ☆ If you could do anything you wanted and were sure you wouldn't fail, what would you do?
- ☆ If you could live anywhere, where would you live?
- ☆ If you could travel anywhere, where would you travel?
- ☆ Before you die, what is it that you want to do, have or be?
- ☆ What's holding you back?
- ☆ What new possibilities wait, right now, on the fringes of your mind?
- ☆ If you continue with your current life choices, what will your future be?

(If you'd like more help with this whole issue of goals and

strategic planning for life

life purpose, check out http://www.gettingagriponlife.com. Robyn has co-authored a very powerful goals toolkit, *Getting a Grip on Life*, to help people not so much with *how* to set goals, but more to help you identify *what* goals you want. It's also an excellent tool with career planning, self-directed appraisals, and life balance.)

Strong leaders have a clear personal vision, as well as clarity in the external areas of their lives, the parts that connect with others.

Leadership lessons

- ☑ Be clear how you want your life to be, and get on with it.
- ☑ Don't sit waiting for things to happen — be a doer.
- ☑ Set goals.

summary of part two

6 All planning is not the same — learn to think strategically

☆ Traditional planning is reactive and backward-focused.

☆ Strategic planning is proactive and future-focused.

☆ Good planning by a committed team can turn around ailing departments — the key goals and clear focus drive change.

☆ Effective strategic planning answers three questions:

Where are we now?

Where should we be going?

How do we get there?

☆ Use a good facilitator and pick a mixed team of different thinkers.

☆ Engage as many members of the organisation as possible: the higher the involvement, the higher the ownership.

summary of part two

7 Twelve steps in strategic planning

☆ Break your 12 strategic planning steps into chunks and they won't overwhelm you.

☆ Keep the wide view — simple solutions may be waiting in the wings.

☆ Follow-through and follow-up are the keys to success — a strategic plan is not an expensive dust collector!

☆ The process must be driven from the top.

☆ Target the most important issues first — don't try to fix everything at once.

☆ Evaluation never stops.

8 Strategic planning for life

☆ Be clear how you want your life to be, and get on with it.

☆ Don't sit waiting for things to happen — be a doer.

☆ Set goals.

part three
the climate

what's it like to work here?
how to build a positive workplace

We've completed two of the four components in the leadership system — foundation, and vision. We've answered two questions: 'Who are you?' and 'Where are you going?' The question now is 'What's it like to work here?' Is your environment toxic or nurturing?

Leaders set the boundaries. They also set the climate and, no, we're not talking about snowdrifts, sunshine and showers. Workers flourish in a good climate and shrivel in a negative one. And it doesn't have to be a high-pressure battle zone out there! Many firms and bosses are terrific to work for. The climate of a workplace is a core component in the leadership system. Some of the effects that flow from this one element of the work environment are:

- ☆ How a person feels about his or her job
- ☆ How much effort is put in
- ☆ How much ownership the person has for his or her work
- ☆ How much flexibility, innovation and autonomy is allowed

Culture or climate?

Before we dig in to this topic of climate, let's get one potential opportunity for confusion out of the way. You might wonder: 'What's the difference between culture and climate?'

part three: the climate

Culture operates at a macro level, climate at a micro level

Culture is the broad brushstroke of how an organisation (a group of individuals) does things; climate is what it's like to work there, and how it impacts on the individual.

Culture is organisational. It's driven by the overall vision, philosophy, skills, history, traditions and the way work is passed on.

Climate is departmental. It's driven by individual leaders and managers, by the way they support and treat all their employees, regardless of status. It varies from department to department and is limited or enhanced by each department leader's ability, values, needs and expectations. Employees can do the job in many places, but they thrive with a leader who knows how to create a great climate.

Climate is a sleeping giant. The job drives *what* people do. The climate drives *how* the job is done.

> *The culture of an international telecommunications company is consistently customer-focused, fast-paced and vibrant. Even though customers and staff experience it from different perspectives, they all have a pretty clear idea of the culture: it manifests externally, it's an overall strategy and image, and it's obvious.*
>
> *However, this same company's climate varies from department to department. David's department suffers from lower morale than Brenda's. Although he works hard to support the company culture, he's a hard taskmaster, doesn't listen to his staff, lacks empathy and has poor management skills. Brenda, on the other hand, has worked hard on her leadership skills, has learned to work with her people in the ways you're about to discover in the next two sections, and has people queuing for a transfer to her department.*

From a survey run by the *Credit Union Magazine* in 1998,

84 percent of surveyed employees said they could do a significantly better job if they wanted to. I don't know what you'd call that, but we see an enormous but silent profit leak! What an opportunity for good managers!

So now, back to you. You're a budding leader, and you want to learn the art of how to create and influence a great work climate. You also want to learn how to help your team grow their self-leadership skills, for you know that a leader's challenge is to spread responsibilities and rewards across all divisions of the organisation — to develop people.

How do you do this, you may ask, and where can you learn?

Not often enough in school, that's for sure! Most colleges don't run 'How to create and sustain a climate of cooperation and effectiveness in the workplace: 101' (although the occasional rare teacher or community-sponsored peer-support programme integrates such concepts into their teaching). And so most of our young people hit the streets with no formal understanding of how to get the best out of themselves, their colleagues and their work environment. Result? Huge loss of productivity, disenchanted staff, and companies who waste incredible amounts of potential earnings.

Do we learn it in our homes? Well — the divorce courts would tell us not often enough! Can we learn it by osmosis? Yes, if we're lucky enough to work in a positive environment, with a great manager. But do a survey. How many of your friends would score their past or present workplaces 100 percent on providing a positive and encouraging work environment?

But it's not all gloom and doom. Even if you're not one of the lucky ones, it's very possible to learn — if you've got an open mind, and are prepared to work at it. Don't expect instant perfection, however. Life is an open book exam, and there's always another valuable lesson waiting just around the corner!

part three: the climate

Mr Grouch's revolving door
The manager of an airport administration team had a hard reputation: he was short-tempered, snappy, intolerant, often grumpy with his people, and didn't seem to know the meaning of the word 'thanks'. In a word, he was a Mr Grouch. The revolving door of his department constantly snapped shut behind yet another disgruntled and departing staff member.

One day his team noticed that he'd taken to reading a book at coffee breaks and lunchtimes. This was no ordinary book — it had a brown paper cover. And when he finished each break it was always carefully locked in his top drawer.

This behaviour went on for some weeks. The curiosity was at fever pitch, but no one dared ask Mr Grouch what he was reading. Then one day, during morning tea, there was an emergency. He dropped his book on the table and dashed out the door.

As soon as his back was turned, people ran for his desk. Sniggering, a bold one flicked it open. To their astonishment the title page proudly displayed How to Win Friends and Influence People *by Andrew Carnegie.*

The book was quietly put back where they'd found it, everyone tiptoed back to work, and nothing was ever said. Over the next few months his bemused and previously skeptical staff watched the transformation from Mr Grouch to Mr Good Boss. It didn't happen overnight, but bit by bit, as he applied some of the principles we're about to outline for you, the whole environment changed. The revolving door stopped swinging, and their department became one of the most popular work choices at that airport.

No matter how bad the present climate, it can improve. If enough of the members of a group (including the boss) shift to a positive outlook, if enough of them apply the principles outlined in the next few chapters, if they develop a shared vision

part three: the climate

and a sense of community, the climate will change for the better. And once enough momentum is created, the naysayers, the negative members, will either adapt or leave. It becomes very uncomfortable for them to stay in their old condition; the 'Law of Attraction' demands that we prefer to associate with people with whom we feel comfortable. (And if you're still left with a recalcitrant bad apple, who stubbornly won't budge and seems to get perverse pleasure from causing trouble, you're well advised to let them go.)

Let's summarise what you're about to learn — for these are the keys to a great workplace climate:

- Be the kind of leader who creates and supports an effective workplace.
- Help your team build a helpful and cheerful environment — happy staff are more productive.
- Ensure that staff feel valued, and are proud to be there.
- Understand how the minds of your people work.
- Know what drives and motivates others.
- Know how to encourage your people.
- Be able to give staff clear instructions, both written and verbal.
- Excel at honest communication.
- Listen actively, with both right and left brain.
- Understand the principles of effective feedback and appraisals.
- Learn to deal with conflict constructively.

We could write a whole series of books on each of these topics, but the purpose of this book is to give you a quick reference check, some quick 'check-the-pulse' pointers as you help your people. (See the bibliography for further study suggestions.)

9
the individual in the workplace

each one makes a difference

In this chapter you'll consider:

☆ How to help your people improve the work climate

☆ Whether you have the right people in the team

☆ Ten keys to enhance the work climate

It's not just the leader of a workplace who sets the climate, but each person within that environment. Inspired leaders are not found only at the top: they can be discovered and developed at every level — and they make an organisation great.

What can you do to help the individuals within your team improve the climate? How can you help them build their own self-leadership and self-management skills? Most of the ideas and suggestions in the next few chapters are good common sense. However, it's a rare person who knows this information intuitively. Most of us can remember a time when we learned it — it seems to come with maturity!

part three: the climate

If you can get inside the shoes of your staff or associates for a minute, if you can understand what the environment is like for them, then, as a leader you'll be able to help them influence their own environment in a positive way. We're not suggesting you become a social worker, for at the end of the day people won't change unless they have a personal interest in doing so. However, an understanding of the happiness, well-being and self-esteem of your team members has a number of benefits:

☆ It will influence the way you handle them.

☆ It will guide you in your coaching of those individuals.

☆ It will highlight issues you as a leader may need to address.

And one other important factor worth highlighting before we dig into the other topics: have you got the right people in your workplace? One bad apple will rot the whole barrel, and dramatically and negatively influence your climate.

Andrew had recently changed jobs. He'd been a very good real estate agent, but the hours didn't suit his young family. Full of optimism, he took a sales position with a manufacturing company.

It was a small firm and two of the three other salespeople had been there for some time. To his surprise, his sales colleagues resented his arrival. It didn't take too long to work out there were jealousies and concerns about whether their commissions would be reduced; they were afraid their territories would be diminished. The two long-serving people tolerated him with a degree of indifference, although if he accidentally offended he found himself on the cold end of heavy-duty freeze treatment. The third one went out of his way to be nasty. He lied, took leads and sales that didn't belong to him, and generally cast a very heavy cloud.

the individual in the workplace

Andrew felt very much the outsider. His overtures were treated with lukewarm indifference. Within a few weeks, as he struggled to learn the ropes with only occasional assistance from Sam, his overburdened sales manager, his self-esteem levels plummeted. The negative voices in his head had a field day. 'Can I do this? Why did I leave real estate? Maybe I was just lucky before and I'm not really a very good salesperson? Should I leave and look for another position, and if I do, will I fail again?'

Eventually he said something to Sam, who replied, 'It's your problem. Sort it out yourself. You're all adults; just learn to work together.'

And so Andrew struggled on. Commissions were low, his wife was getting very worried about how they would make ends meet, and he was most unhappy. He'd just about reached the point of handing in his notice, when one day the CEO happened to find Andrew in the tearoom, on his own as usual.

Murray didn't get too involved in the day-to-day running of the sales team; when the company was set up the three friends who'd started it had set out clear responsibilities and agreed not to interfere in each other's jurisdictions. However, from his office at the end of the corridor he noticed more than the others realised. An intuitive chap, he took a look at Andrew and said, 'We've never had a proper conversation. Bring your coffee down to my office and let's have a chat.'

A bit of skilful digging and probing, and Murray had the story. Unlike Sam, he listened thoughtfully, gave Andrew some encouraging words, and suggested a couple of things he could do to improve his success rate with sales. Over the next few weeks, Andrew noticed that the climate changed. Not only did Sam give him a bit more help, but also initiated a team discussion about territories. Then Murray ran a brainstorm session for the whole sales team and together they identified potential markets they'd not had time to action before (which was why Andrew had been brought on). And the best bit was, the truly nasty guy was dismissed for stealing.

part three: the climate

From then on, as the environment lightened up, so did Andrew's self-esteem. Within six months it all seemed like a bad dream. However, had Murray not quietly intervened, Andrew would have left, bowed down by a sense of failure. (More about how to read the needs of your team, and how to get the right people, in Chapter 15.)

Ten keys to effective employees

As you reflect on the people you're responsible for, consider the following points. A few of them we'll dig into more deeply: others are marker posts for you to investigate at your leisure.

1. Do they understand that our needs drive our feelings, which drive our behaviour and results?
2. What's their level of self-esteem?
3. Are they using, and do they understand, the power of their mind?
4. Do they know how to reframe their thoughts, how to change their internal tapes?
5. Do we encourage people to focus on and increase awareness of their successes?
6. Do they recognise the three Laws for Mental Well-being?
7. Are there gender differences affecting their work?
8. Are their lives in balance?
9. Do they understand their own power sources?
10. Do they have realistic expectations of the role they're expected to fulfil?

the individual in the workplace

The hidden iceberg that drives our results: the **first** key to enhanced work climate

If our basic human needs are not fulfilled, we cannot reach our potential. Instead our attention is focused on survival. Our needs drive our self-esteem or lack of it, which drive our feelings. Whatever our feelings are, so follow our beliefs about ourselves; from there beliefs drive behaviour, which drives results. Everything is interconnected.

Some things are more visible than others, however. Like an iceberg, the first four levels are invisible to others, even if they sense them. Only we truly know our own needs, our sense of self-esteem, feelings and beliefs. On the other hand, behaviour and results are visible.

So, you're a leader with a poorly performing team member? There's a high chance that something important is under the surface, just like the bulk of an iceberg, and the cause of the behaviour you're seeing. The diagram below (Figure 13) may be

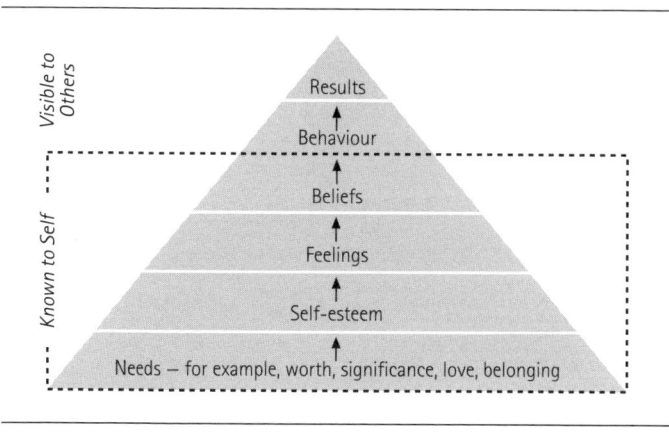

Figure 13 • Needs drive results

Visible to Others: Results ← Behaviour

Known to Self: Beliefs ← Feelings ← Self-esteem ← Needs — for example, worth, significance, love, belonging

part three: the climate

useful as a conversation point, or at the very least as a guide or diagnostic tool for you when you aim to help others. (A different way of looking at basic human needs is outlined in Chapter 15, where we discuss Maslow's Hierarchy of Needs.)

Self-esteem: the **second** key to enhanced work climate

A healthy self-esteem is the first, last and most important quality. It's the rock-solid foundation block on which all personal effectiveness is based. Look at the self-esteem checklist on the opposite page. How do you think each of the people in your organisation measures?

No doubt, as you compared your team members with the list, you saw opportunities for improvement. You have an important role to play in enhancing their self-esteem: your job is to create an environment of mutual respect and appreciation. If self-esteem is so important, how can we, the managers and leaders of these people, help them make personal changes?

Self-awareness on their part is key, and also a willingness to change. Someone who struggles with this issue must be helped gently — a heavy hand will only drive the lack of confidence even deeper. And understand that if poor self-esteem has become deeply ingrained, it will take time to reverse.

Suggestions

Give the people in your organisation the self-esteem checklist to self-mark. Self-identification is more powerful than someone else pointing out our deficiencies.

In an informal chat, perhaps at an off-site coffee shop, find out how they're feeling about themselves, their work, colleagues and the company.

the individual in the workplace

Figure 14 • Self-esteem checklist

15 traits of positive self esteem

☐ I see myself as a valuable and important person, worthy of the respect of others

☐ I feel optimistic about life

☐ I look forward to and enjoy new challenges

☐ I believe I'm an expert (or at very least a specialist) in my field

☐ I don't allow others to feed mental garbage in

☐ I can express ideas easily

☐ I can accept that others are entitled to different viewpoints

☐ I have a clear sense of my own value system

☐ I am confident of the decisions I make, based on the knowledge I have at the time

☐ I expect to reach my goals

☐ I bounce back quickly from temporary setbacks

☐ I take pride in past performance

☐ I hold a positive expectancy of the future

☐ I accept compliments easily

☐ I share successes with others who have contributed to them

(Inspired by Stanley Coopersmith's *Antecedents of Self Esteem*.)

If appropriate, offer coaching, either by yourself if you've got the skills and time or by an independent coach. The coaching industry has come of age: there are sure to be some excellent coaches in your area.

The power of the mind, and how it works: the **third** key to enhanced work climate

Our conscious mind is the larger portion of the brain, but not the most powerful. It processes thoughts, reaches into memory, questions for evidence and logically arrives at answers. The conscious upper brain is divided into two halves: the left side is logical and analytical; the right side is intuitive and creative. The conscious mind gathers information from our five senses (visual, auditory, kinaesthetic or tactile, smell and taste) and is involved in our daily activities. Our conscious mind tells us whether the information we're looking at makes sense or not. According to Tony Buzan, author of *Make the Most of Your Mind*, we access less than one percent of our conscious mind; other experts believe it's five to ten percent.

Our subconscious mind, the smaller, primal part of the brain, lies at the base of the brain. It controls bodily systems such as metabolism, breathing, heartbeat, digestion and body temperature, and *guides* our conscious mind. At least 90 percent of mental activity is subconscious. It functions without us thinking about it. It records our every experience and it holds our emotions. Like a computer, the subconscious takes in information but does not reason; it is impartial, working for or against us, depending on the information we give it.

Not only do we have this invisible workhorse plodding silently at the top of our shoulders, but it's estimated we spend 90 percent of our time thinking about ourselves, weighing and

the individual in the workplace

checking how the events and people around impact on us. So, what's the quality of that inward-focused thinking? What information do we give our subconscious? What internal tapes do we play over and over in our head? The big problem is that for many folk negative and critical self-talk predominates. According to Dr Maxwell Maltz, author of *Psycho-Cybernetics*, at least 95 percent of people have their lives blighted by feelings of inferiority to some extent. For millions this feeling of inferiority is a serious handicap to success and happiness.

How to reframe thoughts, to change internal tapes: the **fourth** key to enhanced work climate

What can we do to stop this 'internal critic'? We change habits by overlaying the old with new. It becomes a conscious choice to play a new message. There may be many things going on around us, but we can only hold one thought at a time, no matter how brief the microsecond. We have the power to choose that thought.

Just as we can change a video or audiotape, so we can change the tape in our head. Surely that's difficult, you might think. No, there are only three steps, and they're very simple. The only hard part is staying with the discipline, and top achievers in every field of endeavour prove it can be done.

The three steps to new thought patterns
1: Evaluate your thoughts
- Who gave me this message?
- What evidence do I have that it's valid?
- What were the motives and needs of the people who gave me these messages?

part three: the climate

- Are my thought tapes about me, or the people I received them from?
- Do I still want this particular thought pattern in my life?

Watch for repeated thoughts like:

- 'What makes you think you're good enough?'
- 'I'm just a loser'.
- 'I'll never amount to anything'.
- 'I've stuffed it up as usual'.

Look to avoid the following thinking patterns:

- Black and white thinking: 'If I'm not the best, I'm a failure.'
- Minimising: 'It was just luck that I passed the bar exam.'
- Comparing: 'I'm not as tall and beautiful as my sister.'
- Mind reading: 'I know you're thinking I should have been here.'
- Critics are always right: 'They must be right, I'm really not that good.'
- Personalisation: 'They didn't talk to me, therefore they don't like me.'
- I feel, therefore I am. 'I feel dumb, therefore I am dumb.'
- The shoulds: 'I should be perfect.'

2: Decide to change

It's as simple as that. Light the fire in your belly that says, 'I don't have to accept mediocrity in my life any longer. I can be all I wish to be. I *will* change.'

3: Overlay the old thoughts, words and actions with more positive ones

For instance, a mistake was made: 'Well, I mucked that one up, but it's a good learning curve. I'll certainly not do that again. What I'll do next time is …' or 'That wasn't like me.'

the individual in the workplace

Encourage people to focus on and increase awareness of their successes: the **fifth** key to enhanced work climate

Many of us were brought up with statements like 'Don't boast', 'Pride comes before a fall', 'Don't blow your own trumpet', and so we rarely praise ourselves, even silently.

That's a wrong message when it impacts on our sense of self-worth and value. Honest recognition of work well done is a very powerful encourager, both internally and from an external source. If we tell ourselves we're doing well, our subconscious will accept it just as easily as those negative words, once it gets used to 'hearing' such thoughts. And a healthy self-esteem is greatly enhanced by a positive attitude.

Robyn's story

Some years ago I was running a programme with the graphics department of a major television company. As a group they had very different personalities from the outgoing sales and advertising people I'd previously worked with — very clever, very able people but much quieter and inward-looking.

As homework I'd asked them to make a list of their achievements. To my surprise, at the next session virtually no one had done the exercise.

'Why not?' I asked.

There was a combined hush. People looked awkward, shuffled in their seats, found it hard to look at me. Finally one person spoke. 'I don't think I've achieved a great deal really. There are lots of people better than me.' Around the room, others nodded in agreement.

I was shocked. And then, one of those magic events that happen from time to time in a trainer's life began to unfold. It must have been divine inspiration, for I'd never done such a thing before, but one by one I asked each person to sit there without speaking and receive

part three: the climate

praise and acknowledgement for their skills and achievements from their peers, plus anything else the speaker wanted to say. At first the person in the hot seat found it embarrassing and difficult to receive, but their colleagues had no trouble in heaping praise and appreciation on them. As each person received the gift of acknowledgement from their colleagues, we all felt love, in its purest form, work magic in that room.

Try it with your team now and then — it's incredibly powerful.

Another idea to help people acknowledge their successes is to implement a peer-recognition programme. Written notes are a tangible reminder of success.

Possible recognition points:

☆ They see someone who goes beyond what's expected.

☆ They want to recognise someone who's helped them out in a special way.

☆ They want to recognise someone who is a positive influence in the department.

Three Laws for Mental Well-being: the **sixth** key to enhanced work climate

☆ The Law of Control

☆ The Law of Expectation

☆ The Law of Attraction

The Law of Control
The more control we feel we have in our lives, the better we feel about ourselves. Conversely, the less control we feel we have,

and the more we feel controlled by outside influences, the less happy we are.

Roman Polanski's movie *The Pianist*, about the brilliant Polish pianist Wladyslaw Szpilman, portrayed this brilliantly. In 1939 the Jews of Warsaw had control over their lives. They were happy, had fulfilled lives and contributed meaningfully to society. As the horror of Nazi occupation built to its awful crescendo, as the Jews were herded like prisoners into the ghetto, then later like cattle into the rail carriages, we saw, we heard, we felt the Jews as a people lose control, lose confidence, lose hope.

Towards the end of the German occupation there were pockets of rebellion by people on both sides of the ghetto walls. We saw the rebels claim back a sense of pride — no matter how seemingly futile, they felt they were doing something.

Law of Expectation

'Whatever we expect we get.' This is called self-fulfilling prophecy.

> *A five-year-old watched as his training wheels were removed from his bicycle. He expected to be able to ride his bike without training wheels. At first he steered awkwardly, wobbling back and forth trying to regain his balance. He rode into the grass and fell several times. When he fell, he picked himself up and tried again. He expected to be able to ride his bike without training wheels and he did ... we're driven to prove ourselves right.*

If our desire and expectation is to enjoy mastering a complex computer program, we'll keep at it until we do. If we expect to find it hard and difficult to master, that also will be true. If we expect to get sick, nature obliges. Have you ever heard someone say: 'I can feel a cold coming on'? Watch and observe — people who say things like this will *always* get what they say. On the other hand, those who feel the same symptoms, but say, 'I'm just throwing off a cold' almost always have a very mild dose.

If we expect to feel inferior, we will. For instance, if you say: 'I don't like going to networking events. I'm not comfortable walking into a room full of strangers', sure enough, you'll feel awkward. Instead, go expecting to meet someone interesting and you'll be amazed what an enjoyable time you'll have. If this feels out of your comfort zone, go and look for someone who is standing alone or who looks uncomfortable. Talk to them and focus on helping them feel at ease. You'll find yourself relaxing also.

Law of Attraction

'We attract into our lives those people, events, good or bad fortune that harmonise with our dominant thoughts.'

Robyn's story
For four years my husband and I lived in Australia. On one of my first trips over there, I made a list of some of the top Australian business people I'd heard of, would like to meet, and wanted to learn from. At the time I knew about 12 people in the whole of Australia, and certainly had no connections with the people on my list. By the time we left, I'd spent time with all of them, and one became a good friend.

If you as a leader understand these three laws, you'll be able to help guide the thinking, language and expectations of your staff.

the individual in the workplace

Gender differences: the **seventh** key to enhanced work climate

We live in a very different and much more accepting environment today than even 20 years ago, but there's still a long way to go. More and more women are rising to the top of major business and government positions, clearly able to hold their own alongside male colleagues. At the same time, men are moving into non-traditional male roles, such as secretaries, home support or house husbands, to name a few.

Then there are sexual variations. Is your workplace accepting of gay men and lesbians? Of people who've changed gender? Check out your own workplace and practices. Is there a true acceptance of differences? Is there understanding of the value of those differences and how to get the best from them all? Or is there subtle undermining, an underlying current and climate of non-acceptance and suspicion. Typically someone who's 'different' has to work three times as hard to be accepted.

For instance:

- ☆ Women tend to be more collaborative in their management style, which can be seen as weakness.

- ☆ A soft, quiet voice in a meeting tends to be overlooked, and the opinions of that person are considered to be insubstantial.

- ☆ A person with a strong voice, or a deep voice, can easily dominate a group.

- ☆ Men are better at concentrated focus, one thing at a time. (And women often interpret this as 'not paying attention', when they ask men to simultaneously consider something else.)

part three: the climate

☆ Women are generally better at multi-tasking. (Men can interpret this as 'flitting from thing to thing'!)

(Everything already said also applies to racial differences, and that *certainly* is another book!)

Are your people's lives in balance? The **eighth** key to enhanced work climate

When life is out of whack, many don't stop to notice until a crisis hits. The signs will usually be there if you take the time to notice.

> *A very dedicated teacher used to stay at work until all hours; there just never seemed to be enough time to do everything. Then one day his wife left him. Instantly he became more efficient with his time, put boundaries around the responsibilities he would accept, and began to have a life outside of work. Sadly it was too late for his own marriage, but from then on his concerned and supportive advice helped a number of colleagues about to fall into the same trap.*

Do you have staff who work too many hours a week? It might be a symptom of an unhappy home life.

Perhaps they think that is what is expected of them. Maybe their time or energy management needs attention. Or do they think they'll get promoted if they work silly hours? How many sick days do they take? Do they spend the first week of an annual holiday with sickness?

Sometimes a manager has to encourage staff to 'get a life'. A burnt-out employee is not a good employee. Also, be careful you don't create a culture that rewards long hours. Month after month, a large IT company gave out the 'Best Player of the Month' award. The recipients were always those who worked crazy hours, who put their family needs to the side in order to work weekends and long evenings. Bad message.

Power sources: the **ninth** key to enhanced work climate

Do they understand their own power? You might like to review Chapter 4 — there we discussed *your* power sources, but of course the same thing applies for your team. Teach staff to access their sources of power:

- task power
- reward power
- personal power
- relationship power
- knowledge power
- spiritual power

Clear expectations: the **tenth** key to enhanced work climate

The central question here is: How can we set employees up for success? Employees don't come to work wanting to do a poor job, but yet we've all seen problems. When new employees come on board we give them a job description explaining their role and responsibilities. However, the job description alone is not enough. So what else is needed? Three things:

☆ Work standards stating how well they are expected to perform.

☆ The performance appraisal showing what areas they

part three: the climate

will be appraised on — include a peer appraisal form if used.

☆ A verbal or written agreement of expectations outlining what they can expect from management, and what management expects from them. An example of areas you can expand in this agreement follows.

All meaningful and positive change starts first in our mind and works its way out. Once your people know and practise this, they'll help to create a climate where not only can you lead effectively but they can also develop as leaders.

Figure 15 • Our mutual expectations

What can you expect from us?	*What do we expect from you?*
Honesty	Honesty
Direct, timely information	Teamwork
Support	Quality rather than just quantity
Fairness	Problem solving
Respect	Positive attitude
Leadership development	Information
Listening	Dependability

Leadership lessons

☑ Leaders are found at all levels of an organisation.

the individual in the workplace

- ☑ Get inside the shoes of your people, and you'll gain understanding to help them control their own environment.
- ☑ One bad apple can destroy the effectiveness of good staff.
- ☑ A poor performer may be struggling with some basic but hidden needs.
- ☑ Self-esteem is the foundation block of happy and productive staff.
- ☑ Use the power of your subconscious to create powerful progress.
- ☑ Invoke the Laws of Control, Expectation and Attraction, and greater mental well-being is yours.
- ☑ Diversity equals opportunity, when accepted and allowed room to flourish.
- ☑ Don't let staff work crazy hours — they'll burn out and not only they but also the company will suffer.
- ☑ Teach staff to access their power sources.
- ☑ Set staff up for success.

10
communication is king!

In this chapter you'll consider:

☆ The art of communication

☆ Three styles: equal, competitive and passive

☆ Outcomes and results of the three styles

☆ The importance of keeping the whole company informed

☆ The three Es of easy effective communication — equal, enlighten, and enlist

☆ How to listen

☆ Feedback

☆ Active listening

☆ A communication checklist

Great leaders create a great climate. They not only understand how to enhance and build their people's self-esteem but they're also great communicators. They maintain an atmosphere of

communication is king!

open communication where colleagues are informed about key issues, listened to, and invited to share their opinions. Great leaders weave both *art* and *science* into their communication.

The *art* of communicating with employees involves mutual respect and openness. A primary function for leaders is to create an expectation of safe, honest, two-way communication.

LaVonn's story: Wilma
Wilma Snow comes to mind when I think of a positive work climate and a brilliant communicator. In my first job after high school, I worked as an on-the-job-trained laboratory technician in a major clinic. Wilma was our laboratory manager and training instructor. She'd had polio as a child and stood less than five feet tall. But as a leader, Wilma towered. Her patience was remarkable. Her energy, encouragement and clear expectations created a work climate where people learned, worked hard and had fun. Communication was open and honest. We could ask her questions. We felt appreciated. There was no doubt in anyone's mind that Wilma was proud of each of us. She was manager, mentor and friend. Her encouragement and support of me continued long after I left the clinic.

Wilma's communication skills:
- *She maintained an atmosphere of respect and open communication.*
- *Employees were informed about key issues.*
- *She not only kept employees up-to-date on what was happening in the clinic, she told them why.*
- *They were relaxed about asking questions.*
- *They were regularly invited to offer opinions, to which she listened with respect.*

part three: the climate

- *When she listened, there was a special energy in the way she listened; employees walked away feeling that what they had to say was important.*

How do you communicate?

Broadly speaking, there are three possible styles of communication: equal, competitive or passive. (The study of transactional analysis, and the book *You're OK, I'm OK* by Thomas Harris will give you an expansion of this way of looking at communication.) As you study the following descriptions, think how you speak to the different people in your life. You'll find the method you choose for each person holds up a mirror to the way you see yourself in relation to that person.

An equal communicator sees him or herself as equivalent to the other person. Equal communication is:

☆ descriptive

☆ thoughtful

☆ respectful

☆ problem-solving

☆ goal-oriented

☆ honest

A competitive communicator sees him or herself as superior, and the other person as inferior. Competitive communication is:

☆ judging

☆ ordering

communication is king!

★ warning

★ threatening

★ preaching

★ criticising

★ blaming

A passive communicator sees him or herself as inferior, and the other person as superior. Passive communicating is indirect and manipulative. Hinting, guilt trips, indirect verbal put-downs or back-biting are used to quietly sway others to their way of thinking. It's hard to know what passive people are thinking and feeling. Passive communication is:

★ accommodating

★ pushing your own feelings down

★ ignoring situations

★ manipulating

Figure 16 • Three ways we communicate

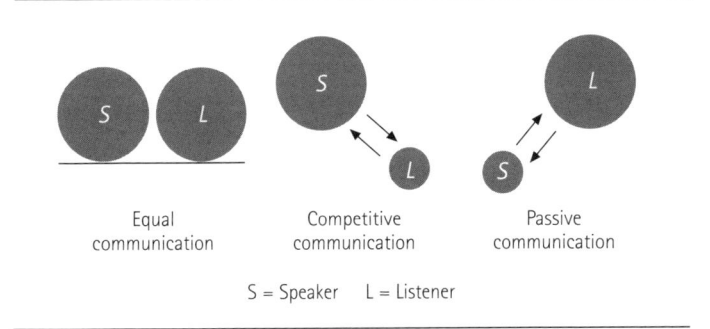

| Equal communication | Competitive communication | Passive communication |

S = Speaker   L = Listener

Figure 16 shows communication as two circles. Notice that equal communicators have speaker and listener circles the same size and the same level. They feel adequate and it shows in their communication.

In a public speaking environment or group communication, this kind of communicator makes everyone in the audience feel as though they're being spoken to personally. They have the skill and congruence to make a genuine connection.

Competitive communicators have their speaker circle larger and higher and their listener circle smaller and lower. Hidden behind the way they bully, blame, demean and take advantage of others is almost always a thinly disguised sense of inadequacy. It shows to the informed observer in their communication style; they, however, may see themselves as being assertive. Bullies almost always have a highly inflated sense of their own importance, a large ego, and a major sense of insecurity.

In a public arena, this kind of speaker causes a discomfort in their audience. Even if at first we're interested, as the minutes tick by we begin to feel patronised, talked down to — as if we don't quite cut the mustard, aren't quite as smart and clever as them.

Passive communicators have their speaker circle smaller and lower and their listener circle larger and higher. They also feel inadequate, but they let competitive communicators bully, blame, demean and use them as a doormat. You'll rarely hear these folk on a public platform — they seldom have enough self-esteem to put themselves up for inspection.

Results of the three communication styles

The result for equal communicators is straightforward communication and fewer misunderstandings.

The result for competitive communicators is that they breed

communication is king!

fear, kill innovation, cause passive-aggressive behaviour and are surrounded by 'yes' people.

The result for passive communicators is that they keep the peace but in the long term feel and cause frustration, resentment and anger. They are not respected by others.

Payoff from the three communication styles

The payoff for equal communicators is mutual respect and open communication. There is little anxiety because they don't feel judged. They get what they want more often because others know what it is they need and want. Equal communication is safe.

The payoff for competitive communicators is control: they get their way.

The payoff for passive communicators is feeling that they don't have to make decisions. Passives withhold their opinions, feelings and wants. They let someone else take the flak for faulty decisions.

Communication: appropriate sharing

The *science* of communication is knowing what is appropriate to share. It's considered and planned for. Determine what employees should know, and keep them informed as much as possible about the overall organisation. The more they hear from you, the less they have to rely on the grapevine.

This is relevant in almost all areas, including customer service, financial matters and even strategic decisions. The major exceptions are particularly sensitive commercial matters and personnel issues. It used to be that employees were given just enough information to do their jobs well. This doesn't work any more. In times of rapid change, employees who know everything possible about the entire organisation are able to understand the organisation's goals and better serve the customers.

part three: the climate

If you can, view the customer service training video *Who Killed the Sale?* It highlights this point delightfully. A manufacturing firm badly needed increased business. The sales team was working with an existing client who was considering the purchase of a much greater range of products. The film portrays a chain of *Fawlty Towers*-style stuff-ups that eventually drove the annoyed and unhappy prospect away. At the finish of the video we see the disgruntled client managing director disappear angrily into the distance. He and his staff had experienced mess-up after mess-up: the final straw was abuse from a company truck driver in the car parking lot. The key point, emphasised throughout, is: keep *everyone* (even the most lowly staff member) informed on anything of importance to the firm.

Even strategic issues, you might ask? Yes, those too. If your team knows what's going on, if you involve them, you'll almost always find they dig in to help to the best of their ability.

Robyn's story
Some years ago I worked as a salesperson for one division of a large building company. The parent company got into difficulties, and the decision was made to downsize our division. Phil Molloy, our managing director, called the whole team into the boardroom.

'I'm sorry to break this news to you, but I've just been given permission to tell you, and I want you to know before you hear it from any other source. We're about to downsize and many of you will lose your jobs. As soon as it's clear I definitely can't keep any one of you I'll tell you, and I'll do everything possible to find you work in another division, if that's what you'd like to do.'

Over the next three months the firm shrank from over 40 people to about four or five. My sales colleagues and I were also on the list. Through the whole process the morale of the firm was incredibly high, sales kept coming in, and no clients were upset. The boardroom was nicknamed 'The Departure Lounge', but camaraderie and good humour prevailed.

The reason for the high morale? More than anything, it was the swift, genuine and compassionate information Phil gave us. We all felt included in the process, we had involvement in our future company placement (if that's what we wanted), and we felt supported and cared for. The grapevine had no chance to breed misinformation, and any one of us, given the opportunity, would have worked for Phil again. He fully earned our respect and admiration, and we worked hard for him right to the end.

The three Es of easy effective communication

Another quick and easy way to remember and expand effective communication is to ask yourself these three questions:

1. *Equal:* do my team and I share mutual respect and open communication?

2. *Enlighten:* do we all understand the purpose and goals of the firm, and does everyone have clear expectations? Is the *why* included in every communication?

3. *Enlist:* do my staff feel a sense of ownership with their work and with the company?

1: Equal communication
Covered by the information earlier in the chapter.

2: Enlighten
Do we all understand the mission, vision and goals of the firm, and does everyone have clear expectations?

part three: the climate

How many employees know the mission of your organisation? How many employees know the vision of your organisation? And how many employees know the company's top three goals for the year? The mission and vision must 'live' in the organisation. When mission, vision, expectations, goals and evaluation are tightly woven together, employees have a common approach to work.

Mission and vision determine goals; evaluation determines whether goals are met or not. Employees linking their work to the mission and vision are anchored to *what* the company is about. Values determine *how* the work is carried out. Your job as leader is to set clear expectations, see that employees do a great job, and celebrate that good feeling of a job well done.

> *We recently ran a course for the middle management of a large aircraft-engineering firm. A much larger international firm had recently bought the company. Perhaps the restructured management had a clear idea of the goals of the newly reshaped firm; however, we quickly discovered that they hadn't filtered down to the workers.*
>
> *Staff appraisals were regarded as an unpleasant chore, so we were there to give them some help. It turned out that job descriptions hadn't been reassessed for some years, recommendations not to advance poor workers were ignored, and there was a lack of clear direction from top management. No one was really sure what the company actually wanted to achieve from the process, appraisals weren't linked to pay assessments, and the people running the appraisals had no idea what happened to the information once they'd done their bit. Our group of mid-level managers were prepared to do them, but there was a blank spot between what they were asked to do and knowing exactly why they were doing it — the purpose of the task. (More about appraisals in Chapter 12.)*
>
> *In another engineering firm, Brett now communicates assertively*

communication is king!

with employees and other team members in an honest, straightforward manner. In the past, he'd had a shotgun rather than a rifle approach to goals and performance. Now, however, he's learned to consciously weave purpose, goals and performance appraisals together. Figure 17 shows how he now connects the purpose, action and expectations.

Figure 17 • Link company mission, vision, values, goals and performance evaluation

Mission/Vision/Values ⟶ Goals ⟶ Performance appraisal

3: Enlist
Ask yourself:
- ☆ In my communications do I enlist and involve my staff?
- ☆ Do they feel a sense of ownership with their work and with the company?

Mutual ownership is a climate where every person counts, regardless of position; where everyone feels they have a stake in the success and growth of the organisation. Mutual ownership happens when employees are involved in decisions, feel free to contribute, and have their ideas listened to and accepted where appropriate. (We're not talking here about company distribution of stocks and shares, although that is an option used in some firms.)

One trap to watch for — never ask for employees' opinions when the decision has already been made. It's a very fast path to

part three: the climate

loss of trust and credibility with your staff. Not only business, but society at large, is dealing with change at an unprecedented pace. There is no way that an old-fashioned 'them versus us' style of manager can keep up with the sheer volume of information.

Peter Drucker, writing in the *Harvard Law Review* in 1988, made the visionary observation that typical large information-based businesses of our time will have relatively few managers, and knowledge will be primarily accumulated at the bottom, in the minds of self-directed specialists.

Effective leaders set an 'us' climate. A manager with an 'I' attitude doesn't get the best out of his or her team. Recently we worked with a woman who overheard her manager say to a client, 'I'll take care of this for you.' The employee was angry — she was doing the work and here was her manager taking the credit. How much better for her manager to say, 'We'll take care of it.' Effective leaders not only change *I* to *We* in thinking and conversations but also teach staff to change *They* to *We*.

One of the most fundamental challenges for a leader is to develop a work climate in which staff can consistently achieve their best. Great leaders weave both *art* and *science* into their communication.

Collaborative questions

Here are some collaborative questions you can work on with your team, as you enlist their input:

- ☆ How can we save time? Time is today's currency. If each employee saves ten minutes a day, in a year's time they'll have saved a week.
  - What can we do to speed up?
  - What can we do to be more efficient?
  - Is there anything we should stop doing?

communication is king!

☆ Customers are the lifeline to the future.
- What will make our service or product more valuable to the customer?
- How can we over-deliver?
- What will customers need five years from now?

☆ Think strategically in all things.
- How can we monitor changes inside and outside our industry?
- What publications and newsletters do we currently subscribe to?
- Who is watching the trends?
- How can all employees get this information?

How to listen effectively — a powerful motivation tool

The number one complaint we hear from employees across the country is 'I don't feel listened to.'

Hearing and listening are not the same thing. Hearing is mechanical: we hear with our ears. Listening is mental: we listen with our minds and our hearts. The listening process involves the speaker who sends the message, the listener who receives the message, the message itself, and feedback that ensures the message was received. Feedback is the puzzle piece frequently missing from the communication picture.

Communication can be complete, partial or broken. Barriers like education, background, experience, beliefs, gender and past relationship with the speaker all influence whether the message is received as intended.

The best listeners:

☆ Listen actively for meaning, without judging.

☆ Listen with both left and right brain.

☆ Ask for feedback.

☆ Apply the three Magic Listening Secrets.

The four listening levels
Non-listener
No effort to concentrate, doesn't hear what is being said, interrupts, goes off on a tangent, wears a blank stare. The non-listener hears but doesn't listen. The ears are functional, the sounds are in the air, but they concentrate on something else. Ask them, 'What was that weather forecast?' and they answer, 'I don't know. I wasn't listening'. We only hear what we listen for — the rest is just noise.

Marginal listener
Hears the sounds but not the intent, misses some words, listens only at a surface level, makes assumptions. The marginal listener is, for instance, an employee at a meeting, lost in personal thoughts. We've all seen it, and sometimes been that marginal listener. The speaker stops, asks: 'What do you think about that?' and with embarrassment we realise all we have is a general perception, but no detail. Many mistakes are made at this level.

Evaluative listener
Hears words, listens for the facts, figures and logic, but is 'emotionally detached'. They miss the intent. They don't connect or engage at a gut level — they lack empathy. They hear the data, but don't read the speaker's body language. It seems as

if everything you say is filtered through a thick sponge rather than a loose-weave transparent cloth. They're typically not open-minded, at least at that moment. When you speak to an evaluative listener you know you're not really heard.

Active listener
They concentrate, suspend personal thoughts and feelings, listen for intent as well as content, put themselves in the other person's place. They're also skilful questioners. They listen for meaning, without judging. They avoid giving advice unless asked for by the speaker.

Use both sides of the brain

Active listeners use both their left and right brain. The left brain is great in logic, facts and statistics, but poor in sensitivity and empathy. The right brain is great in creativity, imagination and emotions, but poor in facts, figures and detail. Switch them both on, as an active listener does, and you've got a far better chance of 'hearing' with all senses, of seeing the nuances, connecting at a gut level with the emotion behind the words, of clicking into the essence of what's been said, of building rapport.

The solely left-brain listener gets the content, but misses the intent. The solely right brain listener gets the intent but misses the content. Listen with both left brain and right brain to get the content and intent and the speaker will feel heard.

Feedback

Always check your understanding, even if you think you've heard the message, and you'll be amazed how often a new light is cast on a message.

A safe guideline: *When in doubt — check it out*. If you get the

part three: the climate

slightest feeling that you may have missed a piece of the message — check. If the interpretation of the message is important — check. If you see a puzzled look on the other person's face — check.

Partial communication is a culprit inside and outside of work.

> *Deb, a ninth grader, told her mother she was going to Fargo (three hours away) for a statewide music conference. She said she'd leave on the bus on Monday at 3.00 and would return on Tuesday at 2.30. She told her mum the general itinerary for the conference, where she'd be staying and gave her the phone number for the motel. Deb left and her mum and dad had an evening to themselves, complete with dinner out.*
>
> *In the small hours of the night, soundly sleeping parents were startled awake by a loud banging on the window. Shocked, they jumped to the window, only to see their irate daughter, suitcase in hand, demanding that the back door be unlocked.*
>
> *As she stormed in, Deb said angrily, 'I told you I'd be home Tuesday at 2.30!' Which 2.30 had never been mentioned! Neither realised the information was misunderstood – the feedback step had been missed.*

How many letters have to be retyped, how many orders resent, how many relationships are broken because the crucial loop of feedback is missing? Take a minute to think of the last misunderstanding you had and there's a better than 50 percent chance that you could have avoided it if you'd checked your understanding!

communication is king!

The three Magic Listening Secrets

☆ Attending skills

☆ Following skills

☆ Reflecting skills

Attending skills

Be present, look interested, be open, relaxed, alert, involved, listen with your whole body. Attending means we put the paper down, turn away from the television or computer. We look at the speaker and give them our full attention.

Following skills

Encourage the speaker through attentive silence and minimal encouragers like, 'Oh?', 'I see', 'Tell me more', 'Really?', 'Go on'.

Reflecting skills

Paraphrase, sum up what you've heard and understood. By doing so you're smoothly inserting a feedback loop into the conversation.

How to kill a conversation dead

- Avoid eye contact.
- Interrupt.
- Run side conversations.
- Complete the sentences of the speaker.
- Clock-watch.
- Do something else when the speaker is talking.
- Walk away.

part three: the climate

Exercise: productive listening habits

From this list of productive listening habits, choose one or two. Use them for the next 24 hours. Each day choose another one or two habits, and continue your practice and focus for at least 31 days. You will improve your listening skills as you work on each habit.

- Listen to an entire message before judging
- Concentrate on what is being said
- Listen for concepts and major ideas
- Overcome distractions
- Focus on the other person
- Listen more than you talk
- Listen in neutral
- Paraphrase
- Clarify
- Use the other person's name
- Return to unfinished business
- Keep confidentiality
- Use intentional silence
- Listen carefully as the conversation closes
- Include each person in conversation through eye communication
- Do not interrupt
- Practise equal communication – levelling
- Let your body support your mind
- Let your ego go
- Be patient

communication is king!

Two habits I will practise for the next 24 hours are:

1 ....

2 ....

Is your communication system working?

Leaders get buy-in from the team by having a well-oiled communication system, and by highlighting what's going well. The more employees know about the organisation, the more they can put their time and energy into the right things. If, at a regular staff meeting, a leader were to ask, 'What's going well?' they'll build pride and personal commitment in their team.

A communication checklist

☆ How fast does bad news travel upwards?

☆ Do your team members ask for help, or do you find out about their struggles only when work isn't up to scratch?

☆ If you were to ask any worker about the strategic direction of the firm, or the reason for major decisions that impact on them, would they have an informed answer, or look at you blankly?

☆ Do staff members feel free to disagree with you, or do you find yourself surrounded by a bunch of 'yes' people who never challenge or question you?

If bad news doesn't reach you until last, if your staff never disagree with you, if your people have no idea of the strategic direction of the firm, it says more about you than it does about

part three: the climate

them. On the Monopoly board of business, pay the banker and return to 'Go'! It's time to start some serious education about effective two-way communication.

Leadership lessons

- ☑ Great leaders are great communicators — they use both art and science.
- ☑ The art of communication involves mutual respect, openness, and two-way communication.
- ☑ There are three broad styles of communication: equal, competitive and passive.
- ☑ The science of communication is about sharing information appropriately.
- ☑ Keep everyone informed as much as possible, including on strategic issues, goals and mission.
- ☑ If your communication enlists and involves your staff, they'll feel a sense of ownership in their work and the company.
- ☑ Don't ask for employees' opinions if the decision has already been made.
- ☑ Effective leaders create an 'us' climate.
- ☑ Hearing and listening are not the same.
- ☑ Effective active listeners are motivational.
- ☑ We only hear what we listen for — the rest is just noise.
- ☑ The left brain listens for logic, facts and data; the right brain for creativity, imagination and emotion.
- ☑ Always check understanding — the feedback loop helps prevent misunderstanding.
- ☑ If in doubt — check it out!
- ☑ Practise productive listening.

11
how the leader impacts the climate

In this chapter you'll consider:

☆ How staff benefits influence climate *and* the bottom line

☆ Why people leave their jobs

☆ How to inspire your team

☆ The four principles of leadership

☆ How to involve your people

☆ How to build on the different operating styles of your staff

☆ How to get full involvement — engage their mind, not just their brawn

☆ Reward the behaviour you want more of — praise to the goal

☆ One person can make a difference

☆ Be a well-balanced EQ and SQ leader

☆ What employees like and don't like in a manager

☆ What employees want from a manager, in order to flourish

part three: the climate

We've already discussed the vital importance of safe, open communication. In this chapter let's take a look at the other key areas you need in order to finely tune your leadership skills. A great work climate influences productivity, morale, teamwork, stress, turnover, retention and recruitment. It's also the best way to achieve excellence and attract and retain top people.

Leaders need the right people in the right jobs in order to reach their goals. Great talent is hard to come by, which makes it even more critical to have a great climate. Otherwise your staff will vote with their feet.

Example of staff benefits and how they impact the bottom line

If you want an amazing example of the way one company creates an outstanding climate, track down a video clip of the TV documentary about SAS, the North Carolina software company privately owned by Jim Goodnight. Since the late 1970s they've experienced hugely profitable double-digit growth. In the US it was the subject of an NBC news clip; in New Zealand it was part of 60 Minutes *in October 2002.*

Here's a sample of some staff benefits:

- *They have four Montessori daycare centres next door to the workplace.*
- *Medical staff provide free medical care, and the company also pays 80 percent of specialist medical bills.*
- *Gyms, pools and other sport facilities, freely available for the staff, are scattered throughout the attractive tree-lined and landscaped grounds.*
- *Nearby top-quality country club facilities are available for staff and families for only $3000; for non-staff the fee is $30,000.*
- *The well-staffed Work/Life Centre has a team of social workers to help employees with any personal issues, including help with extended family members.*

- *Staff are encouraged to work only 35 hours per week, and are welcome to use sporting facilities at any time.*

Their annual staff turnover is three percent, where most other companies average around 20 percent turnover. (If you do the numbers on time and productivity lost with staff turnaround, you'll see an immediate benefit!) At SAS, people line up to get on the staff.

The company focus with regard to all this philanthropy is a drive to find anything that inspires creativity and helps productivity.

Owner Jim Goodnight, when asked why he provided such a huge range of employee benefits, said, 'What's wrong with treating your people well? It's not altruistic — it makes good business sense.'

He believes, and practice bears out his belief, that happy employees equal happy clients. In most companies the benefits are whittled away over time; in this one they keep going up.

He added: 'You have to dare to be different. With public companies it's harder to persuade the shareholders to have a long-term view. Most publicly listed companies suffer the short view. They focus on immediate gain, and completely overlook the invisible profit drain of staff turnover. I shun conventional wisdom. Ninety-five percent of my assets drive out the front gate every evening, and it's my job to bring them back in the morning.'

Why do people leave their jobs?

From a survey done by Stephen Taylor of Manchester Metropolitan University, and outlined in depth in his book *The Employee Retention Handbook*, the main issues fall into the areas of climate and management.

Almost all can be, or are, impacted by the leader:

☆ Bullying, rudeness, lack of respect or abuse of power.

☆ Failure to manage (for example, sweeping problems

under the carpet, avoiding making decisions, refusing to listen to employee grievances, failing to give feedback, failing to show any appreciation for a job well done).

☆ Perceived favouritism — failing to treat everyone in a team the same way.

Taylor also found that a number of problems occur when supervisors are appointed too young. Not only do they often receive little training, but many of them don't have enough life experience to exercise wisdom and good people management. If you're one of those young managers, hopefully the pearls of wisdom in this book might help smooth your path!

There's a further and somewhat invisible problem. Many organisations don't *know* the real reason for staff turnover. People who leave because they've received poor supervision tend not to tell their employers the full story. They're afraid it will jeopardise good references, or burn bridges with people whom they often like personally. So they soften and hide the real reason for leaving; they say it is pay rates, time for a change or personal reasons.

How to make your people feel valued

A positive and productive climate flourishes when people feel valued by their leader. Wilma Snow, mentioned in Chapter 10, applied this powerful philosophy. It's there for the world to see, but so little applied that you'd almost think it was a secret! Many employers and leaders overlook it. So, how can you make people feel valued? Let's take another look at Wilma. Not only did she keep her people informed in the ways we discussed in Chapter 10, but she also inspired and involved them.

Inspiration

Wilma believed that each person is worthy of honour and respect, regardless of status. She believed in human dignity. She believed in her people and their potential before they even believed in themselves. She saw what they didn't see themselves … because she looked for it. She knew how to treat people, understand them and read them, and in doing so, intuitively she inspired them to greater heights. Seemingly without effort she applied four key principles of leading others:

- ☆ She unconditionally accepted people.
- ☆ She made them feel as though they belonged.
- ☆ She encouraged a sense of self-worth in those around her.
- ☆ She believed in people, and people's feelings of competence flourished because of her management skill.

Acceptance: the **first** key principle of leading others

People die trying to achieve this. Ask any therapist, in any discipline, how many people seek help because they feel unaccepted by a parent or someone close. When we can accept people just as they are, warts and all, they sit easy in their body, relax in their spirit, and expand into their rightful place. No one has the power to change another, but by accepting a person just as they are, we can give them the power to change themselves.

Have you ever been in a situation where you feel someone doesn't like you, or you sense they find you unacceptable in some way? Isn't it uncomfortable! Even when the one sitting in judgement thinks they've hidden it, we sense rejection at a

part three: the climate

visceral level. Non-acceptance wounds the spirit. Wilma had the gift of making people feel accepted, not judged. If you need more help with this area, there's a short list of recommended titles in the Resource section.

Here are a few simple strategies:

- Eliminate rigid expectations of how you think another should act or be.

- Don't be critical and fault-finding.

- Don't rush in with remedies for what you perceive as their faults.

- Be open to others' differences — they probably find you 'different' too.

- Listen without judgement.

- Keep a quiet detachment — when we become bound up in 'this is the only way to do this' it quenches the life and enthusiasm of others.

Belonging: the **second** key principle of leading others

We can motivate people by helping them to feel included. This is a step up from acceptance — a higher level of interaction. With the exception of a very few hermits, human beings are designed to 'belong'. We're driven to seek connections — to a family, with friends, our special support groups, our work team, our company, our community, our associations, our neighbourhood, right through to global web-based interest groups. Even the toughest seek a sense of community. No matter how dysfunctional we might think the group is, they seek to belong — look at any gang.

As a leader, how can you foster a sense of community and

how the leader impacts the climate

family with your staff and associates? How can you help them connect with co-workers and have fun? Smart managers find, just as Jim Goodnight does, that if their people have fun together, play together, feel supported, feel they belong, they work better.

Think of the associations or social groups you belong to, or have considered joining. Remember how you felt when you went as a guest to one of the meetings? How did members welcome you? How were you recognised? How comfortable did you feel? Answers to these questions determine whether you joined or not, how involved you became if you did join, for how long you renewed your membership. What lessons can you carry forward from those experiences into your workplace?

Some ideas to increase inclusion (there are plenty more):

☆ Learn spouses' and children's names.

☆ Follow up on family illness.

☆ Be generous with time off for family illness and bereavement. (Seems obvious, but we know an employer who very reluctantly gave their most valued employee time off for her father's funeral, rang her three times during the day, and expected her back at work early the next morning.)

☆ Have baby-picture contests.

☆ Take five-minute doughnut breaks to celebrate employee achievement.

☆ Plan social club outings.

☆ Support internal and external sports events.

☆ Encourage the staff to care about others' welfare.

part three: the climate

☆ Promote volunteerism. Some companies contribute staff time as well as resources to community or humanitarian projects. The Body Shop is one such example.

☆ Celebrate special achievements.

Robyn's story

In the early days of my real estate career I won my first sales award. It was exciting to receive it at an Awards Breakfast with sales peers from the whole group — well over 100 people. However, the best bit was when I got back to the office of the small division I worked for. There on my desk was a huge bouquet of flowers from my boss, and the team (who hadn't been at the Awards Breakfast) crowded round with genuine delight at my success. It was totally unexpected. The impact? I just wanted to work harder for both the boss and the firm. A previous job had not been as successful, but now I really felt as if I belonged, as though I finally had found a work 'family'.

Self-worth: the **third** key principle of leading others

This is the sense that 'I am important'. Cultivate a climate of mutual respect and appreciation, regardless of status. Ask opinions. Listen. Identify and help your employees work from their strengths, instead of pushing them reluctantly into areas in which they have no natural aptitude. Encourage and support them. Focus on people first, then on the task. Create an 'us' climate. (This is also discussed in the previous chapter, in relation to creating a sense of ownership.)

The president of a voluntary association was winding up the monthly meeting. As he went through his regular thank-you list his eyes lit on a quiet woman he had forgotten to put on the list. Month after month she worked at her small but important job, helping to make the function go smoothly.

Just in time he added, with total sincerity, 'And a special thank you to Suzanna. She hardly ever gets a chance to attend the meetings, but she does such a wonderful job that the hotel staff come looking for her every month. It's people like Suzanna who make this organisation the special group it is.'

As he spoke her face glowed as if a lamp had been lit. Such a small thing, so easy to overlook, and so important! Always let people know you value them.

Build competence: the **fourth** key principle of leading others

Ensure that your team know and understand their work and can do it efficiently and effectively. Then expect the employees' best work.

- ☆ Give honest, timely feedback (more in Chapter 12).

- ☆ Reward and recognise excellence (as in Robyn's example above).

- ☆ Develop careers and encourage growth even though this may mean employees will outgrow your department.

- ☆ Provide the resources needed to do the work.

- ☆ Institute a system where employees recognise employees for outstanding work.

Involvement

What other skills have your people got? Many extra skills will be hiding gem-like inside them, including ones they've sharpened outside of the work environment. Have you ever surveyed their interests and hobbies? Where possible, seek to expand their horizons and make use of their skills. It will keep them interested and involved.

They might belong to Toastmasters and have great skills with public speaking. Perhaps they could either train staff who need presentation skills, or even become involved with client presentations. They may have a passion for model trains. Are you utilising their mechanical brilliance at work? They may be talented artists, with a gift for design and colour. Could you invite their advice and help on office image, signage, bulletin board and posters? They may have a fantastic garden and love to design plant layouts: perhaps they would happily design a better landscape around the office. A keen interest in the outdoors, and a love of tramping? Many trampers love sharing with others of like mind. What about a staff outing to a nearby national park?

The marketing manager of a large car firm was a computer enthusiast long before large hunks of plastic decorated every desk. He gladly took on desktop publishing the company newsletter. It certainly wasn't in his job description, and the company could well afford to outsource it. However, Paul really enjoyed the challenge, was happy to learn the desktop publishing program in his own time, and it made his job more interesting.

Understand and tap into the different operating styles of your people

How do they like to receive instructions and how do they like to work? If you don't know, you'll not be able to involve them as effectively. There is an enormous body of fascinating information about personality styles, learning and processing styles, and just what makes us tick as humans. Although we expand on it more in Chapter 15, an in-depth analysis is far beyond the scope of this book. It's a well-recommended journey that could take the rest of your life! You'll find some recommended titles in the bibliography.

Two related areas of study are Howard Gardner's seven styles of intelligence, and various behavioural sciences, especially the rich study of NLP (Neurolinguistic Programming). Gardner's seven styles of intelligence are: linguistic/words; logical/mathematical; musical; kinaesthetic; spatial; interpersonal/relationships; intrapersonal/self. If you're struggling to connect with someone, it may be that their dominant intelligence style is very different from yours.

NLP is a huge topic. If you choose to study it in depth you'll find yourself embarking on a lifetime study! Let's take just one brief example from NLP, to whet your appetite for further learning.

There are five sensory ways in which we process information:

☆ Visual.

☆ Auditory — breaks into subsets of auditory tonal: hearing and sound; and auditory digital: making logic and meaning of something through the written word.

☆ Kinaesthetic or tactile.

☆ Olfactory or smell.

☆ Gustatory or taste.

Almost all of us will have a dominant or preferred sense through which we understand instructions and information, and access some or all of the other senses at various levels and times.

part three: the climate

Our preference in how we like to receive information and instructions can have a dramatic impact on the way we work and how we interact with and involve our colleagues. If we don't understand this, the potential for miscommunication and frustration is quite high.

Maureen was the marketing manager of an IT company. She was a fast-thinking, fast-speaking, bright, alert young woman. She packed an amazing amount into every day, was very efficient, a great manager, and was well liked by her team. Her preferred way of receiving and processing information was visual — the fastest processing method.

William was her graphics guy, very clever with design, a whiz on a Mac, and turned out great work. He was primarily a tactile, or kinaesthetic, learner/processor. It took him a little longer to understand instructions, not because he was slow, but because kinaesthetic learners need a gut connection before they can 'hook up' with information. They find it difficult to 'get a grip' on requests when someone talks too fast, or they're expected to pick up complex information with one quick explanation.

Neither he nor Maureen understood this. The outcome? They regularly frustrated the heck out of each other, despite their appreciation of each other's skills and genuine liking of each other. In a training course this issue of preferred processing styles came up.

For the first time Maureen understood that she needed to slow down in her instructions, give William time to connect with what she was saying, not overload him with too much at one time, and give him a chance to integrate. She finally understood that it was okay if he took a little longer to complete a task — he would turn out great work if he weren't rushed.

William finally understood that Maureen wasn't trying to confuse him when she issued instructions at 100 miles an hour. He realised he

how the leader impacts the climate

could ask her to slow down and she wouldn't think he was dumb and stupid. He now had enough confidence in himself to query hard deadlines. And with this new knowledge there was enough confidence and goodwill between them that if it really was a tight deadline she could explain and he would push himself to meet it.

As these distinctions and others flowed, they looked at each other with a mix of shock and delight. At last, an explanation for what had been happening! From then on their combined productivity dramatically increased. Work became even more enjoyable, and the already positive climate in the team notched up several degrees higher.

Engage their mind, not just their brawn

Are you interested in getting full and involved participation from your people? Instead of telling someone to do a task, ask them how they think it should be done.

According to Les Giblin: 'It is psychologically impossible for a human being to give us 100 percent of his brawn, unless he is also allowed to give us his ideas.' The following story is taken from *Investors' Reader* of September 1951.

In 1931, Christmas at Baltimore's McCormick & Company was the sad affair it had been for years. Notices were given of a layoff 'until about February 1' along with the ironic wish of 'Merry Christmas and a Happy New Year'!

In 1950 the employees of McCormick & Company's Baltimore plant worked pell-mell right up to the day before Christmas, then left for home with a whoop and a holler. And no wonder: in their pockets was two weeks' extra cash bonus and ahead of them a full-paid winter vacation until January 2. The bonus was in addition to three weeks' extra already paid that year; the vacation was in addition to the regular summer vacation and seven paid holidays.

part three: the climate

The contrast between these two situations is the degree of success achieved in less than 20 years by one man and one idea. The man is perceptive 55-year-old Charles Perry McCormick, chairman and president of 'the world's largest spice and extract business.' The idea is 'multiple management', an operating system designed to ensure maximum worker participation and morale, to say nothing of providing management with a seedbed of youthful and ambitious executive talent.

The story starts back in 1889, when Charlie's uncle, Willoughby McCormick, started his spice business in a dingy room with two employees. 'Uncle Will' was a hard worker and a hard boss. Sales reached $3,500,000 in 1932 but employees were listless and dispirited. Labour turnover was an expensive 30 percent each year.

Nephew Charlie (the 'Old Man' had no children) started working at the plant in summer 1912, and came on full-time in 1919. He worked as stock boy, runner and executive assistant in factory and office, and for over ten years as salesman and export sales executive. He also tried to sell Uncle Will some new management ideas but was fired seven times for his trouble (he was also rehired). Then came the Great Depression and big losses for McCormick. As was the tenor of the times, the Old Man slashed wages 25 percent and had another 10 percent axe in hand when he suddenly died on a business trip in 1932.

Since it did not seem to make much difference who headed the hard-pressed concern, the directors elected young Charlie. The practical prophet decided to use some of his ideas. He called a meeting of all employees and announced a 10 percent raise instead of a cut, and a work week shortened from 56 to 46 hours. He also told the workers they had to raise production and cut costs or the whole kit and caboodle might collapse. To help them along he told his astonished employees they would henceforth share in the profits of the company and take an active part in management.

how the leader impacts the climate

> *The active part consisted of a junior board of directors and the beginnings of multiple management. The first board had 17 members (credit clerks, cost accountants, assistant department heads). Their assignment was to find ways and means to improve anything they thought needed it. Charlie added: 'Write your own constitution and by-laws, elect your own officers and govern yourself as you wish. The company books are open to you and ask all the questions you like.'*
>
> *To keep things under control, Charlie said all suggestions must be unanimous and subject to approval of the senior board (the stockholder board elected annually).*
>
> *The idea clicked. Within a few years the junior board had redesigned and modernised the company's packages with a resultant sharp rise in sales; they devised new ways to test stenographers; they introduced faster and better billing; they suggested new product lines from pumpkin pie spice to the recently introduced fast-selling cinnamon sugar.*
>
> *As a good spice man, Charlie likes to say 'the proof of the pudding is in the eating'. On that basis the junior board has quite a record: of 5000 suggestions made, over 99 percent have been adopted by the senior board. Says Charlie: 'I cannot estimate how much these suggestions have meant to this company in increased sales and profits but certainly the benefits far exceed the cost'. More important, the junior board has bolstered morale and given all ambitious young men a chance to be a company officer and director. The goal is attainable since no less than 13 of the present 17-person senior board were formerly junior or factory board members.*

(Note: Also reproduced by Les Giblin in *How to Have Confidence and Power in Dealing With People*.)

Another more recent and world-famous example of a similar experience is outlined in *Maverick* by Ricardo Semler. By involving his staff in a number of unconventional ways he turned the company he inherited, on his father's death, into one of Latin America's fastest growing companies — and it was a time of savage recession. If you're interested in stretching your mind on this topic, we strongly encourage you to read the book — it's a great read.

Reward the behaviour you want more of — praise to the goal

Whatever we focus on enlarges. So, if we want people involved and engaged in the organisation's goals, put the attention there. Praise them when they perform well, minimise your attention on activities you don't want them to focus on, or behaviour you'd prefer them not to engage in. Praise releases energy, criticism kills it.

A nine-year-old lad was frustrating his mother beyond belief. Every time she asked him to do some perfectly innocuous task, all she got in return was grumbling and complaints. Refrains like 'It's not fair', 'It's Maurice's turn', 'I didn't make the mess', 'I don't want to' echoed round the house. In the midst of her frustration, one day she realised she'd begun to sound as cranky as him.

In desperation she suddenly remembered hearing about Positive Parenting. In a nutshell, if you reinforce desired behaviour and ignore or give as little attention as possible to unsatisfactory behaviour, the bad behaviour is supposed to diminish. She was clear out of ideas so decided to give it a go.

She picked a calm moment. 'Jimmy, I'm not happy about the way you complain every time you're asked to do a chore. And I'm not happy about myself either — I'm beginning to sound like you! I've had a better idea.

'Every time I catch you not complaining when you're asked to do

something, you'll get a star. We'll keep a list on the fridge. When you've earned 10 stars, you get an ice cream. And if I forget to notice that you haven't complained, you're allowed to remind me, so we can get those stars up there as fast as possible.'

Jimmy took up the suggestion enthusiastically, his mother remembered to praise him to the skies the first few times he willingly accepted a task, and amazingly quickly the habit became reinforced. After three ice creams they forgot to keep track, and it was never an issue again.

Your colleagues might be wearing bigger shoes, but try it — the principle works just fine with adults too!

One person can make a difference

All workers, at every level, want credit and recognition for work done well. Not only does it make them feel better, but they are actually able to do more. And it doesn't have to be a manager or leader who gives the acknowledgement.

Carol Price, an American trainer on self-esteem, on her tape series How to Present a Professional Image, *tells the story of a young girl who worked for a restaurant chain. This young lass was not very confident, so to shift her focus off her own low self-esteem Carol encouraged her to embark on a programme of thanking and acknowledging her fellow workers. This included writing them notes and sending them little cards.*

She was fairly new in the company — a humble waitress. About a year later, the company managers came to visit this particular outlet. They wanted to know why this restaurant's results were consistently better than other outlets.

All enquiries pointed to this young girl. By her positive, genuine appreciation of her colleagues, she had lifted their morale. This flowed on to the customers who enjoyed their eating experience more, spent more money, and no doubt recommended the restaurant to others.

The young woman was promoted to a management position, and given a healthy pay rise.

Be a well-balanced EQ and SQ leader

For many years we've talked about IQ as a measure of intelligence. We've lauded the folk who registered high, and yet some of those incredible brains have been very dysfunctional humans. In the last few years writers and thinkers have realised there's a lot more about humans that can and should be quantified, measured and used as guide posts. They've realised that a human being doesn't just need an able brain, but also emotional (EQ) and spiritual (SQ) intelligence. And so they've come up with new terms for information that's probably been discussed since we stopped chasing mammoth herds!

Solomon was right — there's nothing new under the sun! But it's wonderful to see the business world becoming aware of something beyond budgets and balance sheets, payrolls and productivity. 'IQ allows us to think, EQ helps us relate, SQ allows us to do both in times of rapid change,' says Margot Cairnes in *Approaching the Corporate Heart*.

Emotional intelligence (EQ)

This covers self-awareness, self-management, social awareness and relationship management. It's the ability to read and regulate emotions in ourselves and others. Those with high EQ are motivated, self-disciplined, aspire to excellence, continually seek reskilling, enjoy learning and look to add value. You'll find a company with high EQ people has a strong corporate culture, high morale and low staff turnover. Daniel Goleman is one popular author on this topic. There's been quite a bit written about the topic, so we won't take time here to overview it. You'll find it well worth the study.

Spiritual intelligence (SQ)

This involves spirituality, but not religion. Nor is it about esoteric practice used only by a few. Instead, it's about robust and practical spirituality, one relevant to those of all faiths as well as those of no faith. It covers how to integrate ethics, integrity, authenticity and wholeness into your whole life, including business. It's based on our current understanding of how the laws of the universe work.

As SQ is just beginning to receive mainstream acceptance in the business world, let's take a couple of minutes to dig a bit deeper. The SQ approach to leadership covers three key aspects:

- ☆ A clear, well-articulated vision that is understood and embraced by the people.

- ☆ It is strongly values-based.

- ☆ It is able to uplift and inspire people by engaging their hearts, mind and spirit.

The following values, when grounded in truth and emotional honesty, contribute towards building strong teams that harness the best of people. Through positive role modelling and by providing a framework of clear expectations, people are compelled to give their best back.

The six core SQ values

Doing no harm

Businesses do not exist in a vacuum. They exist within communities and as such, SQ leaders must ensure that they are respectful of the people and environment and not contributing harmful and toxic side effects — socially, environmentally and emotionally.

Respect and dignity towards others

Leaders often have to make hard decisions. SQ leaders ensure that there are systems and processes for dealing with these and that they are fair and reasonable. It is a humbling and heartening experience when an employee says, 'This is personally very hard for me but the company has treated me very well in how they ...' When we lose respect and dignity for others, we lose our humanity.

Authenticity and alignment

SQ leaders are totally aligned with who they are and what they say and do. They are able to 'walk the talk'. Their congruency factor, a barometer of honesty in effective communication, is high and others immediately respond to this. They are good role models of leaders who really live out what they believe, in an 'inside out' sense.

Contribution

SQ leaders view their role in a much larger framework than immediate job satisfaction. They are less about ego and more about having a framework of contribution, making a difference and operating from a base of servant leadership. Questions such as 'Who am I?' and 'How best can I serve others?' are clear and pretty well resolved in their minds and hearts.

About 2000 years ago Lao Tze wrote: 'Enlightened leadership is service, not selfishness. The leader grows more and lasts longer by placing the well-being of all above the well-being of self alone.'

Self-knowledge, learning and growth
SQ leaders operate from a model that encourages learning, growth and development in self and others. They're open to feedback and actively seek self-knowledge, which further enhances their understanding and management of those around them. There is permission for team members to 'try out' new approaches, and mistakes are viewed as learning opportunities.

Good character and conduct
There is harmony between their thoughts, words and deeds, fostering high levels of trust. People know where they stand. Think about it for a minute: without trustworthiness, leaders don't really last too long.

(With thanks to Jasbindar Singh, of SQ Consulting [www.sqconsulting.co.nz] for this overview.)

What employees don't like in a manager

The top three complaints of employees are:

- ☆ I don't feel listened to.
- ☆ I'm not respected.
- ☆ Others try to control or manipulate me.

What employees want from a manager, in order to flourish

According to research by James Kouzes and Barry Posner, employees want managers with these traits:

- ☆ Honest

part three: the climate

- ☆ Forward-looking
- ☆ Inspiring
- ☆ Competent

From our research we'd add:

- ☆ Open
- ☆ Consistent
- ☆ Respectful
- ☆ Accepting

Top leaders build an atmosphere of trust and credibility. This is found when there is congruence between what we say and what we do, where we demonstrate competence, where we care. Are employees commonly enjoying these characteristics in their managers? Not often enough, according to what we hear. If we want involved employees, managers need to bridge the gap in trust and credibility.

Here are specific comments and recommendations for management we've gathered from employees over time:

- Tell us your expectations and reward us when we exceed them.
- Reward the behaviour you want more of.
- Encourage us.
- See our talent before we do.
- Let us know you believe in and trust us.
- Catch us doing things right.
- Make it safe to ask for help.
- Seek our opinions — we're at the frontline and often have good ideas.
- Communicate 200 times more than you presently are!

how the leader impacts the climate

- Give us responsibility and hold us accountable for results.
- Set goals *together*.
- Write notes thanking us.
- Do it now. Only five percent act on requests within 24 hours.
- Ask for opinions and advice *before* you've made your decision.
- Relate to the person first, then to the task.
- Listen to us.
- Celebrate progress together.
- Treat people right regardless of status; no one is better than anyone else.
- Spend time with each of us as individuals.

If you're up for an opportunity, ask your employees:

a) how they'd like to be treated (your information gathering might be more successful if you ask an independent consultant to gather it)

b) to score the following questionnaire.

Exercise: employee satisfaction audit

Use the following letters to indicate your answers beside the questions: Y = yes; N = no; S = sometimes

How do you rate your work environment?

☐ I know what is expected of me at work.

☐ I have the materials and equipment I need to do my work right.

☐ At work, I have the opportunity to do what I do best every day.

☐ My fellow employees are committed to doing quality work.

part three: the climate

- [ ] In the last seven days, I have received recognition or praise for doing good work.
- [ ] My supervisor, or someone at work, seems to care about me as a person.
- [ ] There is someone at work who encourages my development.
- [ ] In the last six months, someone at work has talked to me about my progress.
- [ ] At work, my opinions seem to count.
- [ ] The mission/purpose of my company makes me feel my job is important.
- [ ] I have a best friend at work.
- [ ] This last year I have had opportunities at work to learn and grow.
- [ ] I receive clear and unambiguous information all or most of the time.
- [ ] I receive ongoing communication – not just in times of crisis or need.
- [ ] I receive information before, not after, important events.
- [ ] I'm able to give feedback on issues.
- [ ] All my two-way horizontal and vertical communication lines are open and clear.
- [ ] I am given timely information about issues affecting my organisation, job, and responsibilities.
- [ ] I know why the organisation adopts its policies and procedures.
- [ ] I know about the organisation's community activities and am encouraged to contribute to civic and community projects.
- [ ] I have a good overview of how our products or services are received in the marketplace.

(Source: an amalgam from an in-depth Gallup Organization study, and 'The Employee Communication Bill of Rights' from *The Practice of Public Relations* by Fraser P. Seitel.)

how the leader impacts the climate

In these last two chapters we mentioned Wilma Snow, a woman only known in her own workplace. She's not a famous person, but she's inspiring. Let's finish with another inspiring leader, this one somewhat better known. None of this is complex stuff, and there's nothing new under the sun, but if it were common practice we'd have had no need to write this book!

Southwest Airlines is famous for its positive work climate. Herb Kelleher, their CEO, has a management style the employees love. He's a great motivator.

Since its beginning in 1966, Southwest Airlines has modelled how to hire the best people, set high expectations, get results and have fun while doing it. Morale is high and employees are friendly and attentive. They like their work. Southwest has grown from a regional airline to the nation's fifth largest airline and has consistently shown a profit. Herb gives employees credit for the strides Southwest Airlines has made.

Since 9/11, other airline carriers have suffered a huge loss while Southwest Airlines has continued to make a profit.

Leadership lessons

- It's good business sense to treat your staff well.

- Staff turnover is an invisible profit drain.

- Ninety-five percent of your assets drive out the front gate every evening. It's your job to bring them back in the morning.

- The leader impacts almost all the reasons people leave their jobs.

part three: the climate

- ☑ People who leave because of poor treatment tend not to tell their employers the real reason.

- ☑ A positive and productive climate flourishes when people feel valued. It's their perspective that counts, not our intentions.

- ☑ Inspiring leaders accept unconditionally, help people feel they belong, and build self-worth and feelings of competence in others.

- ☑ Find out the interests and hobbies of your staff — you may be able to involve them more.

- ☑ Work out the different intelligences and sensory processing preferences of your staff and you'll find it easier to get good results.

- ☑ Don't just tell someone to do a job: instead, ask them how they think it should be done.

- ☑ Whatever we focus on enlarges.

- ☑ Praise releases energy — criticism kills it.

- ☑ Everyone wants credit and recognition for work well done.

- ☑ 'IQ allows us to think, EQ helps us relate, SQ allows us to do both in times of rapid change.' — Margot Cairnes.

- ☑ Employees want managers to treat them with respect and courtesy — and not enough managers do.

12
feedback, criticism and appraisals

In this chapter you'll consider:

☆ More on how you as a leader can provide feedback

☆ Bonus tips on how to criticise and correct

☆ How to run successful appraisals and performance reviews

In the questionnaire at the end of Chapter 11, how did you and your organisation measure up? If there's some scope for improvement, decide on priorities, set a goal to seek answers, and keep reading! Some of your answers may be in this chapter.

How to give effective feedback

Work from strengths, yours and others. Look for opportunities where employees can showcase their talents.

When good work is done, make sure your staff get the glory, even if it was your idea in the first place. As mentioned on page 124, bosses who hog the limelight and take credit for other people's work instantly lose credibility and respect. They become a laughing stock, once people get over being mad. On the other hand, leaders who quietly step back, pushing others forward when it's time for the accolades, earn huge respect and loyalty from the people they lead.

Much feedback is too general or too vague to be helpful. The following six simple rules are guidelines for both praise and criticism. (And because criticism and correction are feedback 'hot spots' we'll cover them more deeply, further in the chapter.)

Figure 18 • Essential steps for effective feedback

Praise	*Criticism*
Praise the behaviour	Criticise the behaviour
Do it soon	Do it when relevant
Be specific	Be specific
Tell the person how you feel about it	Tell the person how you feel about it
Stop for a moment of silence	Stop for a moment of silence
Encourage more of the same	Encourage the behaviour you expect

Praise/criticise the behaviour

Focus on behaviour and results, not on the person; impersonal feedback is far more effective.

If we praise the people instead of their actions we run the risk of inflating their ego, instead of increasing their skill and job-related self-esteem. Another potential problem is that some people read praise of themselves as insincere.

Most employees have responsibilities in four broad areas: service, accuracy, timeliness and 'selling' (products, service, image,

feedback, criticism and appraisals

credibility). You might use them as beacons in your search for excellence.

If you need to criticise, it's even more important to keep personalities and personal attacks out of the conversation. For example, instead of 'What were you thinking! You were stupid to say such a dumb thing to that client,' try something like, 'It's a good idea not to say … to clients.'

Do it soon/Do it when relevant

The quicker we praise, the greater the impact. Remember in school when you took tests? Weren't you interested to see how well you did? You looked for the grades within the next few days. If they were late they lost their punch. Other events and tests had taken prime spot in your mind.

With criticism, choose your time. Sometimes that's as soon as you pick up the mistake, especially if something has to be corrected, or if you might forget, or the same task won't be done again for some time.

However, if possible wait until the next time they do the same task and then quietly give the correction. If people have done their very best, by criticising when they've just finished you take away their sense of achievement. It's kinder to say, as they're about to do the task again, something like: 'You did that job very quickly last time, thank you. One thing I'd like to add, which would improve the result, is …'

Be specific

You may have been told, 'You're a good employee.' I guess it's better than not hearing anything, but what does it mean? What is good?

Overheard in a corridor: 'You've got a rotten attitude.' What does *that* mean? Such a comment is no help to the employee.

What can they do to improve? If you don't tell them, they can only guess.

Tell the person how you feel about it

This is especially important with criticism. Don't point the finger, you'll attack their ego. Instead, express how it impacts on you.

This is one case in communication where you put yourself in the forefront of the story, as you take responsibility for your feelings instead of laying blame. It doesn't make the person wrong; it just means that you don't like something, which is a much less adversarial stance. You'll find it often takes the heat out of a potential argument.

For example, 'When you argue, I feel very uncomfortable', rather than 'You shouldn't argue'. (A good strategy for personal relationships as well as work ones; try it when you're lining up for a domestic disagreement!)

With praise, it makes a stronger personal connection between the two of you.

For example: 'I really appreciated you doing extra time last Thursday. We couldn't have finished year-end inventory on time without you.'

Stop for a moment of silence

Let your message sink in. Most of us are not comfortable with silence: we rush to fill the void. However, a pause is powerful; it is a very effective way to make your point. Quiet yourself for five seconds after you've told the person how you feel, especially when you criticise.

Encourage more of the same/Encourage the behaviour you want

Behaviour encouraged gets repeated; don't focus on what you don't want.

Bonus tips on how to correct and criticise

Start from a positive perspective
When improvement is needed, be specific and redirecting, but always work from a positive perspective. For example, 'This department is very good at timeliness with order processing. The GM is keen to implement our systems throughout the company. Where we can improve is management of our paperwork once the order's gone.'

Keep your purpose in mind — beware blame and justification
The real purpose of criticism is to achieve a better result. If we attack someone's ego we drastically reduce the chance of getting the desired result. They're so busy fighting a rear-guard action that the root of the problem frequently gets overlooked.

Give them loopholes
Leave them room to save face if they change their stance. Otherwise they have to defend their previous position. Few people, once they've taken a strong stand for something, are able or willing to admit that perhaps they're wrong.

Two possible loopholes are:

☆ Assume that they didn't have all the facts when they started. This gives them an excuse for having been wrong. Start with something like: 'I can understand how you came to that conclusion.'

part three: the climate

☆ Give them a chance to lay blame elsewhere. It's a rare and very big-spirited person who's prepared to own up to all their faults! For example, an accountant in your company has missed out some important figures in a balance sheet. You draw their attention to the omission and they say, 'No one told me I had to include those.'

You know they were told, and the procedure manual explains it in detail, but they obviously haven't read it lately (if ever). If you give them a hard time you achieve nothing — they won't want to admit they forgot. Instead, you could say, 'Well, it's in the manual, but perhaps one of the other staff took it home.' (Sure, isn't it everyone's favourite bedtime reading!)

The guideline is to constantly think, 'What is the goal I wish to achieve here?' If the soft way will achieve what the hard line confrontation won't, choose the soft way. Take a long-range view: you want the job done right the next time, by happy staff. Ask yourself: 'If I come down hard and heavy here, if I embarrass them, will I achieve my objective?'

Don't blame others to make yourself feel better, more important or justified

This is one of the most insidious problems in relationships and communication. Small-minded, short-term thinkers blame others for their problems and mistakes. Open-minded, positive people take responsibility for their own actions, and find constructive ways to work round problems. Which are you?

Give praise sandwiches, not blame bullets
Toastmasters know that criticism wounds people's spirits. So, in order to help would-be public speakers learn their craft, they apply a wonderfully simple formula after every speech: CRC — *Commend, Recommend, Commend*. The recommendation for improvement comes sandwiched between two slices of praise. Positive outweighs potential negative 2:1, and the improvements are quietly inserted by the evaluator as recommendations rather than criticism.

Criticise in private
Never embarrass people in front of their peers. If you deflate their ego like a pricked balloon (and you will if you criticise in public), you literally close their ears. They become physically unable to hear anything else you say, which is not an effective strategy if you want them to change their behaviour.

Supply the answer — this isn't an exam
The emphasis should be on the solution, not the mistake.

Ask for cooperation nicely
A demand for assistance puts people's backs up. Polite requests imply the feeling that they have a choice, even when the staff member really knows they have none. Leadership is the art of getting people to do what you want, because they want to.

Don't nag — one criticism to an offence
Once an issue is dealt with, don't keep dragging it up. All you'll do by revisiting a mistake is create antagonism.

Let the final memory be encouraging
Finish any correction in a positive way.

part three: the climate

A quick guide on how to run successful appraisals and performance reviews

Most people dread appraisals and reviews, and so put them off until the last minute and totally misuse or under-use them. When used well, though, appraisals are a very positive tool to acknowledge success, review an individual's progress and help people increase their skills with a planned learning and career path. And a good appraisal system makes the company more productive and profitable.

The main problem with annual appraisals is leaders who don't manage their own time and process. It's not the staff member's fault if it's done badly. With a positive mindset and attention to the five matters below you'll find it an enjoyable part of developing your team.

Here are five reasons why appraisals are not popular:

- ☆ The forms are too subjective.
- ☆ It's seen as a task, not a process.
- ☆ The people doing the appraisals aren't confident in their skills.
- ☆ Feedback and coaching is seen as extra work, not an integral part of the job.
- ☆ Fear that it may create conflict. It's seen as something done *to* them rather than *with* them.

The forms are too subjective

Most review forms are not designed to objectively address people's performance. Therefore it almost forces the reviewer to make a subjective assessment. It becomes 'your opinion versus mine'.

Review the questions on your forms (you may have to take

the issue up with your HR or Personnel department). What objective questions can you ask, so that desired performance is clearly understood, observable and able to be commented on in a constructive way?

You may need to vary the scoring scale. For instance, 'Manages Health and Safety issues well' probably only needs a *Yes* or *No*. A scale of 5 or 7 would normally be too fine a variation.

It's seen as a task, not a process

A good leader reviews performance continually. Do informal performance appraisals every four to five weeks so employees know what they're doing well and what they can improve. Unfortunately, many leaders see the appraisals as a time-consuming annual event that adds no real benefit to the organisation. If it's done only once a year, they're probably right!

When ongoing reviews are a natural part of the internal communication, the annual process should be a breeze. It is then only a formal recording of what both leader and staff member know, and are already attending to.

The people doing the appraisals aren't confident in their skills

If they're not comfortable with the process, get them some training (and other hot spots for improvement may come out of it at the same time).

Remember the aircraft engineering firm we mentioned in Chapter 10, who were being trained on how to run effective appraisals? The spin-off was that the brainstorming and sharing with other managers brought out a smorgasbord of connected matters. Because there'd been a gap of some years in the process, some managers lacked the skills and confidence; the forms needed a bit more work; and the top management were not giving clear enough direction. We worked on the first area, and the other matters were relayed to senior management and Personnel: they then worked on the recommendations relevant to their areas of responsibility.

Feedback and coaching are seen as extra work, not integral to the job

If you're this far into the book, you don't need any further comment on this! For some individuals, sadly it's true! Anyone who believes this is not a true leader, in our opinion. Instead they're managers of output, not leaders of people. Beware of getting bogged down in your area of expertise and forgetting about the people for whom you have responsibility.

Fear that it may create conflict

If the first four matters haven't been attended to, who knows what surprises might jump out and bite you! Use objective questions, support your team with ongoing review and feedback, and your risk of conflict is minuscule. And if it does come up, well, it needed to be attended to anyway.

Of course, if you've got a difficult person to deal with, there's a high possibility of conflict. (The next chapter might give you some new tips on how to handle it!) Putting it off isn't going to improve the situation, and if it's that bad, you need to deal with it smartly, probably well before an annual review.

Two cardinal appraisal rules

☆ *Never* surprise employees with what's in a performance appraisal. If they're surprised with a bad comment, you've definitely not done your job. Any problems should have already been talked about and hopefully already handled.

☆ *Involve* staff in their appraisal. Employees should be responsible for tracking work and bringing evidence.

Give them the appraisal form beforehand, ask them to score themselves, and *then* have your meeting. You also review the questions beforehand so you're prepared, but the actual completion of the form is done together, in a conversational way. Nine times out of ten, they'll mark themselves harder than you would. Then you've got the happy task of pointing out what they've done well, as well as assisting them positively to move forward on a clear track.

Your forms probably also have a section for further goals and development. By giving them the form in advance they've had time to think about what they want, instead of doing mental gymnastics in your appraisal meeting.

Here's another really successful strategy. In addition to the final appraisal form, ask them to answer these four questions:

☆ What were they most proud of during the past year?

☆ What were their major disappointments?

☆ What could have been done differently?

☆ How can you help them do a better job?

Leadership lessons

- Look for opportunities for employees to showcase their talents.

- Leaders ensure that accolades are given to their staff, rather than themselves. By doing so they earn huge respect and loyalty from their staff.

part three: the climate

- ☑ Leadership is the art of getting people to do what you want, because they want to.

- ☑ For effective feedback:
  Focus on behaviour and results, not the person.
  Praise quickly: correct when appropriate. (It may be just before they do the task the next time.)
  Be specific — non-specific comments are a waste of breath.
  Take responsibility for your feelings, instead of laying blame.
  Don't point the finger — you'll attack their ego.
  Use silence — a pause is powerful.
  Focus on the behaviour you want, not what you don't want.

- ☑ Correction:
  Start from a positive perspective.
  Don't attack their ego.
  Give them loopholes.
  Don't blame others to make yourself feel more important.
  Use the CRC praise sandwich for effective improvement.
  Criticise in private.
  It's not an exam — supply the answer.
  Don't nag — only one criticism to an offence.
  Finish any correction on a positive note.

- ☑ Appraisals:
  Ask objective questions, instead of ones that force a 'your opinion versus mine' response.
  Review constantly and informally — then it's a breeze.
  Get employees to rate themselves first — most of the time they'll be harder on themselves than you would be.
  Do appraisals *with* staff, not *to* them — the appraisal is an opportunity for two-way feedback.

13
how to deal with conflict

In this chapter you'll consider:

☆ Three techniques to handle angry complaints

☆ How to deal with conflict

☆ A diagnostic to protect yourself and your team from unethical people

Wouldn't it be lovely to live in a perfect world, with no problems or complaints? Hmm, well, it ain't gonna happen! And here's another angle: complaints and difficult people are a gift — they highlight an area of potential improvement. Generally it's only people with high self-esteem who will register a complaint or cause you a problem; the quiet ones slide away into obscurity, giving you no chance to correct the issue.

Three techniques to handle angry complaints

First, let them have their say, and don't interrupt. This one action will defuse about 50 percent of potentially volatile situations.

Second, pause for a moment, then connect with empathy.

Say something like 'I can see how you would feel that way'. It shows the other person that you have listened to them instead of working out your answer while they spoke.

It also gives you time to calmly consider the best course of action. Most people don't handle silence very well. Often the one who speaks first compromises, as they have less self-confidence.

Finally, draw them into the solution. Don't rush in with solutions, or excuses.

Don't take it personally. In almost all cases the person is unhappy about an event or an action, not you personally. The focal point is 'What can we do together to prevent this from recurring?' Then do it quickly.

How to deal with conflict

Not all conflict is bad; like complaints it can be a spur to improvement. But, handled badly it can not only impact the morale in your organisation, but also affect the bottom line.

Be flexible. Don't take a hard, non-negotiable line. Our natural response in an argument or disagreement is to justify ourselves. If we defend ourselves and argue back, battle lines are immediately drawn, and the chance of a satisfactory solution is greatly reduced. Don't let ego get in the way of a satisfactory solution. Look for win-win solutions.

A TV interviewer was chatting on air with a woman selling perfumes. He tried to politely tell her that some people didn't like the promotional perfume strips placed in magazines. They found their whole magazine was overwhelmed with a perfume not of their choice. The viewers could see letters and comments from readers in his hand.

The woman just looked him straight in the eye and totally denied that it was possible. She took such a black-and-white stance that there was no chance of a half-way point, of agreement, of acceptance that some folk may have different value judgements than her about her product. Perhaps she thought she was defending her product. To the viewers she became increasingly silly; it threw everything else she said into grey shades of doubt.

Don't exaggerate
Be moderate, accurate and fair. If you express the possibility that you may be wrong, it often turns others round.

Respond quickly
If you've agreed to take action on something, follow through swiftly. It helps to repair relationships.

Bottom-line consequences
When people are distracted by negativity, you'll find systems, processes and productivity slow down.

Customer service and sales are frequently impacted. Unhappy staff members won't give their best to the person on the other side of the counter, the phone or the desk.

There's a danger of internal sabotage
Disagreement and problems handled quickly are only a conversation. Left too long, conflict escalates from daily events to challenges to battles.

Why do we try to avoid conflict? For many, it's because they don't know how to manage it productively. There's a paradox here: as we learn to welcome and manage conflict, so we will suffer less from its consequences. Fear of conflict freezes us; action releases us.

part three: the climate

Robyn's story
Many years ago I was a leader for a young mothers' support group. Quite unwittingly I upset one of my committee members. She didn't know how to handle it, but told one of her friends, who then took it upon herself to let me know. I was horrified to find that I'd upset Liz; I felt sick in the stomach, didn't sleep, and worried about it like a dog with a bone. This state of anxiety went on for a few days. Finally, plucking up all my courage, I rang her.

There didn't seem any point in beating around the bush, so straight to the point, I said: 'Liz, I'm very sad to hear I've upset you. I do apologise — I had no idea that what I said as a throw-away line would be so inappropriate.'

It was the last thing she expected to hear. At first she was embarrassed to find that her complaint had been reported. I assured her I wasn't upset about hearing; I was upset that I'd distressed her.

Then she put herself in my shoes. To my surprise, I found myself being praised! The injured party became the supporter!

'Thank you so much for calling. I don't think I would have been brave enough to do what you've just done. I'd have been so mortified.'

The best learning was, as soon as we began to talk, the knot in my stomach went away. The days before I picked up the phone were far more stressful and distressing than what came after. Ever since then, in both a personal and business context, I've been a believer in cleansing the wound of any misunderstanding as quickly as possible.

Steps to resolve conflict
- Notice it.
- Decide on your goals in relation to the issue.
- Step back and identify why it's occurring.
- Plan how you'll raise the issue, and how you'll lower barriers.

- Anticipate the possible problems and have a Plan B.
- Discuss it with the person or persons concerned.
- Get agreement from all parties to resolve it, if at all possible.
- Find a satisfactory resolution.
- Keep it relevant. Don't get lost in past issues.

Notice it
Many people never address conflicts because they don't want to admit that they exist. Recognition is both an emotional and a mental state.

Decide on your goals in relation to the issue
What do you want to achieve? There are usually five possible outcomes. You may not want all of them — it's important to stay focused, or you may find yourself completely out of the game! Possible goals are:

☆ To understand the other person.

☆ To be understood.

☆ To get resolution to the conflict.

☆ To get commitment from the person to take certain actions.

☆ To help the person understand the consequences of the current circumstances.

Step back and identify why conflict is occurring
Conflicts occur for many reasons, including misunderstandings, differing goals or methods, power and control struggles, different

values or beliefs. If you have some idea of why the issues have arisen, you're in a more powerful negotiating position. According to Christopher W. Moore in *The Mediation Process*, there are three main sources of conflict:

☆ Relationship conflicts (emotions, misperceptions, poor communication, differing values).

☆ Data conflicts (lack of information, relevancy of information, interpretation of information).

☆ Structural conflicts (time constraints, role definition, unequal resources, unequal power and authority).

Plan how you'll raise the issue, and how you'll lower barriers
If you can start in a non-threatening, inclusive way you'll tumble barriers. You might start with something like: 'Anna, I know that you are frustrated with …. Can we talk about why you think that's happening?' You're looking for ways to build a bridge from which to communicate, ways to build rapport.

Use questions, but also give enough information so it doesn't seem like an interrogation. As much as possible, keep the focus on finding out what exactly the issues are. Be careful to avoid 'fluff' or 'story', which digresses and sidetracks. Questions such as 'What specifically do you think would fix the problem?', or 'What do you think is the underlying issue behind the matter?', or 'So what's the *real* issue here, do you suppose?' help to direct the conversation.

Anticipate the possible problems and have a Plan B
In your mind anticipate how you want the meeting to go — future pace it. Mental rehearsal of positive outcomes increases your chance of success.

how to deal with conflict

Also, step into their shoes. How are they likely to behave? Do you think they'll be defensive, aggressive, domineering? If you can stay focused on your goals and not get sidetracked by your emotions or the actions of the other person, you're in a very powerful position. If you've anticipated and already considered how you'll manage the situation you're far less likely to be caught on the back foot, compromising on issues you'll later regret.

Eileen, a part-salary, part-commission salesperson, asked for a meeting with Ruth, her boss. She had a false view of her value to the firm, and believed she was a useful staff member. In fact, over a three-month period her sales hadn't covered her salary, let alone created any profit for the firm. When Ruth pondered the reason for the meeting request, knowing Eileen was a poor money-manager, she came to the conclusion she was about to badgered for a pay rise.

Ruth was a very fair-minded and generous person. Typically she'd bend over backwards to help someone in difficulties, often to her own detriment. This time, something bothered her. She began to realise she was being played for a sucker.

She stepped back from the situation, giving a lot of thought to the future of the company. Her husband had just been transferred to another state. The initial plan had been to build the firm up to a stage where it could be run from a distance, and Eileen was hoping for that opportunity. But now another option occurred to Ruth.

On the due day, Eileen turned up, with her friend Matthew for support. The two of them persuasively laid out her case. Sure enough, a pay rise was the objective. Nothing was said about the value (or lack of it) that Eileen delivered; the whole case was built around her inability to manage on the money she earned. Eileen and Matthew came to the end of their presentation and sat back, expecting their rhetoric to turn up the dollars.

part three: the climate

However, Ruth had gone into the meeting with a plan.
Quietly she sat back. She paused; the silence grew.

'Thank you for suggesting this option, Eileen. However, I've decided to change the company direction. I'm selling and moving to be with my husband. I'm sorry, but I have to give you notice. I already have a buyer lined up and there won't be a job for you.'

The greedy pair sat back on the cushions, their mouths open. As they stumbled down the stairs, still in shock, Ruth realised a huge load had rolled off her shoulders. But, she also realised she could easily have been bulldozed into a very messy and money-draining situation if she hadn't taken time to be well prepared.

Discuss it with the person or persons concerned

Too often we talk about the conflict to everyone but the right person. Once you're in dialogue, use these three steps. They will help you quickly engage in conversations in as non-threatening a way as possible.

1. *Use an 'I' message* — it states what you see from your perspective and allows for the possibility that you could be mistaken. 'I' messages can be:

   - those that reveal what you think or need, such as 'I think', 'I believe', 'I have decided' or 'I would like'
   - those that reveal what you feel when confronting conflict.

   The confronting 'I' message has three parts: I feel _____ (emotion), when you _____(other's behaviour), because I _____ (consequence of the behaviour).

2. *State the issue to be addressed* — this lets the other person know exactly what you wish to discuss.

3 *Request a conversation* — this shows that you're serious: you really do want to have a conversation.

Examples of non-threatening conversations

- *Revealing your thoughts or needs*
  'Harry, I'm concerned about the pay process. Could you go over it with me later?'
  'Andrea, I have decided not to work on the budget committee this year. Can we find some time to talk today?'

- *Confronting conflict*
  'I feel concerned when you miss deadlines because it's putting the team behind on this project. Can we talk about this?

Get agreement from all parties to resolve it

If there's a common goal to reach a solution, you're more than halfway home.

Seek a satisfactory resolution

Ideally you're looking for a win-win resolution. However, it's not always possible. Sometimes it has to be a compromise, and that may be acceptable. What's not acceptable is someone who tries to force their opinion and views, to dominate the conversation, effectively turning it into a win-lose situation. Allow the other person to retreat with dignity.

If people feel heard and respected, you'll often find they can live with compromise. A positive resolution should also include follow-up plans to make sure that the conflict stays resolved.

Sometimes you may decide to let the conflict run, to do nothing. The important thing is to be objective and clear, and to understand the implications of your action or non-action. There are times when an unhappy team member will leave if you do nothing, and that's the perfect outcome. If that's your chosen path, just remember to think ahead, anticipate any damage control that may be necessary, and be prepared for possible negative fallout.

They may threaten you with unfair dismissal and legal action. Check your legal standing, follow due process, and if they still threaten the law, let them. Even if you have to pay a premium to get them out of your company, you'll save money. A negative or unhappy employee can very quickly destroy a business. It may seem unfair that you have to pay to get rid of them, but the cost of keeping them will be far higher.

(There are many excellent and comprehensive books and courses on conflict management, negotiation and arbitration. As with other subjects in this book we've given you enough to deal with regular business situations. If you're struggling with a serious conflict situation, you'll get value from further study or help from professional negotiators and mediators.)

A diagnostic to protect yourself and your team from unethical people

What we've discussed so far are situations where people are basically reasonable, and there's goodwill to seek and implement a fair solution. However, occasionally we have the misfortune to come across unethical people who have no intention of being fair and honest.

Take a look at the following checklist (Figure 19). If you find yourself with lots of ticks on this list, author Shannon Goodson's solution is: 'Place your hand firmly on your wallet or purse and slowly, but deliberately, **back** towards the door.'

how to deal with conflict

Figure 19 • Unethical checklist

- [ ] Compulsive name dropping
- [ ] Inappropriately calm and poised — even when caught in a lie
- [ ] Being caught in a lie is explained as a 'harmless misunderstanding'
- [ ] Melodramatic use of righteous indignation to over-assert character, credibility, values, integrity
- [ ] Strategic use of actual (or implied) intimidation
- [ ] Few long-term or deep-seated relationships
- [ ] Concealed history of legal problems and financial 'misunderstandings'
- [ ] Difficulty showing genuine emotion, so fakes it
- [ ] Deals with shady ethical issues by justifying them with phrases like 'It's just how you look at it' or 'Everybody else does it'
- [ ] Uses self-delusion to justify unethical behaviour ('You'd do the same thing if you were in my position')
- [ ] Talks long term; thinks and acts short term
- [ ] Features simplistic, manipulative techniques to gain rapport and advantage
- [ ] Considers interpersonal influencers like charm and endearment more important than skill-based competencies
- [ ] Relies on words like 'integrity', 'openness' and 'trust' to deflect requests for proof of character
- [ ] Uses verbal ambiguity as a manipulative technique
- [ ] Behaviours tailored to appear psychologically open, strong, caring and resilient
- [ ] Tainted view of the motives of others
- [ ] Expert knowledge of the tools and techniques used by other manipulators
- [ ] Seems unmoved by threats of being exposed
- [ ] Claims expertise in an unrealistic, impossible number of fields

Source: *The Psychology of Sales Call Reluctance, Earning What You're Worth In Sales*, by George W. Dudley & Shannon L. Goodson, copyright 1999, Behavioral Sciences Research Press, Dallas, Texas, all rights reserved. Reproduced with permission.

part three: the climate

If you've ended up with people like this in your orbit, get them out as fast as you can. No matter how good your leadership, relationship or communication skills, nothing's going to change them — they're out to con you. (Sometimes they're such good con merchants they've conned themselves: they even believe their own publicity.)

Leadership lessons

- Complaints are a gift — a chance to correct and improve.

- To deal with angry complaints:
  Let them have their say.
  Pause before you speak, then use empathy to connect.
  Draw them into the solution.
  In almost all cases it's not you personally they're unhappy with.

- To deal with conflict:
  Don't back yourself into a corner — look for a win-win solution.
  Don't exaggerate.
  Act quickly to correct a problem.
  Disagreement and problems handled quickly are only a conversation; left too long, conflict escalates from daily events to challenges to battles.
  Fear of conflict freezes us; action releases us.
  Many don't address conflict because they don't want to admit it exists.
  Decide your goals in relation to the issue.
  Work out why it's happening.

how to deal with conflict

Be non-threatening and inclusive in your dialogue.
Anticipate problems and have a Plan B.
Use the 'I' message.
Allow the other person to retreat with dignity.
Be prepared to let a seriously unhappy person go.
Dismissal may be the best and cheapest option, even if they take legal action.

☑ Beware of manipulative unethical people — get rid of them as fast as you can.

14

how to get the message not only delivered but also understood

In this chapter you'll consider:

☆ The best medium to make contact

☆ How to write clear business communications, including email

Have you ever tried to get hold of people and they just never seem to get back in touch? Or they're incredibly tardy? Perhaps you're using the wrong medium.

Which medium is best?

In large departments it's not uncommon to have four generations working together. Older employees usually like to talk face to face; younger employees usually prefer email and instant messaging. Then you've got phone, fax, written memos and letters.

The key? Find the preferred medium for the person you wish to reach, and as much as possible use it. Communication is what is received, not what is sent, so it's no good grumbling because

how to get the message not only delivered but also understood

you haven't had a response. Maybe they haven't received it, or haven't received it in a format that they easily connect with. Communication is enough of a minefield without putting unnecessary blocks in the way.

Robyn's story
The new practice manager of one of my legal clients asked me to contact him at a certain date. I'd already done a considerable amount of work for them, they were very happy with the results, and discussions had been afoot for the next round before the change in personnel.

At the pre-arranged date I phoned. A few days later I called again, then left it a week or so, and called again.

And again! And again (all this spread over a period of about two months)! I couldn't work out what was going on, but correctly (as it turned out) put it down to the new man still settling into a very demanding job, and left it a while. However, I was getting a little concerned. How often do you lose a good client because a new person, with whom you don't have the relationship, chooses another supplier? Then, just on a fluke, I tried an email.

'Dear John, not sure if my messages are being delivered, but just wanted to touch base as you'd requested. Thought that perhaps it might be easier for you to respond to email. How's the planning going for the next time management course?'

Within an hour, back came this reply: 'You're right; you've got my attention now! We're not ready yet, but thanks for making the effort to keep in touch, and we'll talk soon.' Subsequently we worked together on a very large staff-training project.

Effective leaders express themselves clearly with the written as well as spoken word. So, as we finish this section on climate in your workplace, let's take a quick look at one last communication tool: how to write better.

If you need to dig more deeply into this topic, or your skills are less than Grade B+, there are excellent courses on letter and business writing. We strongly encourage you, as a leader, to sharpen them. In today's knowledge- and information-rich world a poorly written communication (including emails) sends a louder message than maybe you realise. Poor grammar, spelling, sentence construction and verbose language all suggest to the reader that the writer either doesn't care or has a low level of education. Is that your chosen leadership image?

Email

Mention email these days and you usually hear a collective groan. However, it's an incredibly useful convenience tool when it's used well. If you're not using email much, one day you will, or be left behind! Let's take a quick peek at how you as a leader can ramp up your email writing skills.

We all have horror stories of misuse, but instead, let's focus on some benefits:

- ☆ Easy communication in different time zones.
- ☆ Great for short, informal messages.
- ☆ When used well, and controlled, can save a lot of time.
- ☆ Helps people stay connected when travelling.
- ☆ Makes flexible work practices, such as working from home, possible.
- ☆ Great for the times you need a paper trail, instead of informal conversations.

how to get the message not only delivered but also understood

- ☆ International business is much easier.
- ☆ Saves huge dollars and time in instant transfer of documents.
- ☆ Rapid response (if you got a quick respondent at the other end).

So, with all these benefits, why do we love to hate it? Apart from the deluge of rubbish, and the potential for time wasting, a major reason is the potential for misunderstanding because it's written poorly. We've all had them: a cryptic little note, or a wordy one, scooting down our email system. It leaves you thinking, 'Just what do they mean?' Because email is a flat medium the risk of misunderstandings is high. There are no voice nuances and often no chance for immediate discussion.

Or, a newsletter by email, alias an e-zine, offers good information, but is often boring and lifeless. And we all know what happens with boring newsletters — a rapid 'Delete'. How do good e-zine writers make their writing interesting? Read on!

How to write clear business communications, including email

Some people are very good at communicating in the written form. What are the secrets that improve our readers' understanding, rather than cloud it? (You'll find that many of these points relate to anything written, including marketing pieces, advice to clients, and hard copy as well as electronic.) Good writers ask these five questions:

- ☆ What am I trying to say?
- ☆ What words will express it best?

part three: the climate

☆ What image or images will make it clear?

☆ Is my language fresh and clear? Or is it fluffy, imprecise language and hackneyed phrases?

☆ Can I say it with fewer words or less complex words?

Simple clear language

Keep it simple. Journalists are taught to write for a reading age of 10 or 11 years. Flowery language is not good writing. It's tedious, harder to follow, and lazy on the part of the writer. In fact, concise writing is harder, and takes more time (until you become practised). Mark Twain is reported as saying: 'I'm sorry this is such a long letter. I didn't have time for a short one.' The areas to watch are:

☆ The complexity of the language — use plain, expressive words.

☆ The number of syllables in a word — this is not a test of your wisdom and knowledge. Use simple words.

☆ The number of words in a sentence — less is usually best, but vary them.

☆ The number of sentences in a paragraph — keep the eye engaged, and you'll keep the mind engaged.

☆ The language — is it active or passive; engaging or boring; plain or over-fancy; precise or space- and time-wasting? (And there are more tips in Figure 20 on page 192.)

Try these sentences for size. The first two are from *Managerial Communication*, a university textbook one of our children had the misfortune to inherit as a set text.

how to get the message not only delivered but also understood

A supervisor's receptiveness or willingness to listen to subordinates' ideas, problems, and concerns will improve the motivation of subordinates. Through such receptiveness, supervisors develop knowledge of areas in which they need to provide additional training or explanation in order to build expectancy that the worker can perform tasks.

Why couldn't they just say something like:

A good supervisor listens to the ideas, problems and concerns of their team. Benefits? Higher motivation from the workers, because they're listened to and helped where needed, and bosses who know what's really going on.

Once you get into the habit, it's quite easy to pick too-fancy language and long, boring sentences. However, if you'd like help and there's no one around to guide you, you've got it right there in your computer. You'll need to use your word processing system; this feature isn't in most email programs. On the toolbar, select: Tools, Spelling and Grammar, choose Options, and check 'Show Readability Statistics'. When you've finished writing your piece, run the spelling and grammar check. (It's sometimes a bit of a nuisance; just 'Ignore' all the things you don't want to change.) At the end you get the readability rating. Check the Help menu for more background information about readability, or if your system is configured differently and these instructions don't work.

Be succinct

The more you waffle, the harder it is for your reader to get your meaning. Say what you want to say, and then skip back and take out all the surplus words and sentences. Short, punchy words and sentences engage the reader. For example:

part three: the climate

As she was going into the cafeteria yesterday, Susie decided to stop off at the office and collect the documentation the sales manager had told her about, for the new client

or

Susie picked up the new client documentation yesterday.

Don't use five paragraphs when one will do. You'll find people won't reply to your mail. It's put in the too-hard basket, left to the last, swamped by the next day's deluge.

Create small paragraphs
Use plenty of space, especially with emails. Next time you get an email with no paragraphing, and with more than about four lines, notice how much harder it is to read.

Write as you speak
Even if you're just writing quick work-related emails, make them easy and enjoyable to read. It doesn't take much more time, and helps to compensate for your absence. Be personal and friendly, even in longer pieces — electronic or hard copy. It's good writing, enjoyable to read, and therefore an effective use of time for your readers. Also, your potential audience will read your words before they read wordy, dense, long-winded stuff. Everyone's busy; the easy read gets the eye.

Tell stories
This isn't so relevant for a quick email note, but tell stories in a newsletter article, e-zine or marketing piece. Stories are alive, they're real, and your readers will feel as though they're there. They connect a thousand times more than if you give them bland boring facts and data, even when written well. Think back

to the last really good speaker you heard. I bet they wove stories and anecdotes into their presentation.

Do a spell and grammar check

There is nothing more frustrating to a literate person than poorly spelt and ungrammatical emails, especially when writers are using their first language. (We're all more forgiving of second language users.) Turn on your spell check, so you at least have the choice of making a bad impression. Tools, Options, Spelling, choose 'Always check spelling before sending', and 'Suggest replacements for misspelled words'. You always get the choice to add your own words to the dictionary.

Print off to check

Even the most experienced writers will print off something important before they send it. Your eye sees different things on a hard copy; although we can compose on a screen, it's very dangerous to proofread there.

The other really useful thing, especially if it's an important document, is to write, proofread a hard copy, make changes, leave for an hour or so, then re-proof your document. You'll almost always see improvements.

You might like to keep a copy of the handy guide in Figure 20 (on the next page) near your work station.

Examples: good and bad writing

Here are two jargon-filled phrases, followed by 'plain English' versions. Remember that word-smithing is not an exact science. Your versions would almost certainly not be the same as ours, but if you used the guidelines in this chapter they'll have to be a lot better than what you see below. Clear, easy-to-understand writing becomes easier with practice, even if you're not naturally comfortable with it. The key is to

part three: the climate

Figure 20 • Writing tips for managers

Use active voice
Passive: It was proposed by the planning team that each department set action plans for reaching the quota.

Active: The planning team proposed that each department set action plans for reaching the quota.

Guide the reader
Use transitions, e.g. 'the first ...', 'the second ...', 'the third ...', 'the final'. Use a word or words to link the first sentence of a new paragraph with the last sentence in a previous paragraph.

Use short words
utilise	use
prior to	before
disclose	show
endeavour	try
in the event	if

Use parallel structure
Unparallel: Each department was asked to set action plans after deciding who would lead the team, and meet again in three weeks.

Parallel: Each department was asked to set action plans, select a leader, and meet again in three weeks.

Lead with the main point
Avoid backing into your sentence, e.g. 'Believing that problems can be avoided, I am developing vacation schedule guidelines.' This sentence keeps you waiting until the end to find out what I am talking about.

Keep the reader focused
Sentences of 15-22 words.

Paragraphs of 10-15 lines.

Fewer words or lines are fine, if it creates impact and clarity.

Use headings.

Use lists and bullets.

Use indented paragraphs.

Edit unnecessary words
at this point in time	now
consensus of opinion	consensus
few in number	few
until such time as	until
free prize	prize
advance reservations	reservations

Avoid clichés
it has been brought to my attention
per your request
play it by ear
by leaps and bounds
I couldn't care less

Stay reader-centred
Put yourself in the reader's place. Write to their understanding.

Edit writing
Edit for typing, spelling, punctuation errors, omitted words, fragments, and overuse of adjectives.

how to get the message not only delivered but also understood

be watchful about irrelevant and cluttered jargon. Become the 'Word Police' on your own and others' work.

1. *Another interpersonal response is rejection. This response indicates that 'I care about you as a person, but your behaviour is not consistent with my expectations. I will be happier with you if you change your behaviour to more productive alternatives.' The pressure is on the individual to change his or her behaviour to once again receive the confirming relational messages. Relational messages of rejection must contain a provision for self-correction. This is the important key to giving negative feedback. In later sections, and in subsequent discussions of conflict management, this concept will be addressed again.*

(From the same tedious *Managerial Communication* text mentioned above – it abounds with dreadful examples!)

Possible abbreviation:
Rejection can be a useful tool if someone is behaving in a way you don't like. It says: 'I care about you, but I don't like your behaviour. Sort it out, if you want to get back in my good books.' We'll expand the point later, but the key is to be clear how you want them to improve.

2. *Objective consideration of contemporary phenomena compels the conclusion that success or failure in competitive activities exhibits no tendency to be commensurate with innate capacity, but that a considerable element of the unpredictable must invariably be taken into account.*

Thanks to George Orwell's excellent essay *Politics and the English Language* for the gobbledygook above. He flipped the centuries to show that our modern tendency is to complicate and confuse. (We haven't improved since he wrote his essay in 1946!) Following is his source material, in its beautiful simplicity.

part three: the climate

I returned and saw under the sun, that the race is not to the swift, nor the battle to the strong, neither yet bread to the wise, nor yet riches to men of understanding, nor yet favour to men of skill; but time and chance happeneth to them all. (Ecclesiastes 9:11)

Leadership lessons

- Find out which medium is preferred, if you want to be heard: phone, fax, email, text, written memos or letters.
- Communication is what is received, not what is sent.
- Effective leaders express themselves clearly with both the written and spoken word.
- Poorly written communications imply that the sender either is poorly educated or doesn't care.
- Write in a crisp, clear, interesting way.
- Stories bring a document to life.
- Mark Twain: 'I'm sorry this is such a long letter. I didn't have time for a short one.'
- Be concise: your message will be more easily understood.
- Proof, proof, proof.
- If it's important, proof a hard copy, not on the screen.

summary of part three

9 The individual in the workplace

☆ Leaders are found at all levels of an organisation.

☆ Get inside the shoes of your people, and you'll gain understanding to help them control their own environment.

☆ One bad apple can destroy the effectiveness of good staff.

☆ A poor performer may be struggling with some basic but hidden needs.

☆ Self-esteem is the foundation block of happy and productive staff.

☆ Use the power of your subconscious to create powerful progress.

☆ Invoke the Laws of Control, Expectation and Attraction, and greater mental well-being is yours.

☆ Diversity equals opportunity, when accepted and allowed room to flourish.

☆ Don't let staff work crazy hours — they'll burn out and not only they but also the company will suffer.

part three: the climate

☆ Teach staff to access their power sources.

☆ Set staff up for success.

10 Communication is king!

☆ Great leaders are great communicators — they use both art and science.

☆ The art of communication involves mutual respect, openness, and two-way communication.

☆ There are three broad styles of communication: equal, competitive and passive.

☆ The science of communication is about sharing information appropriately.

☆ Keep everyone informed as much as possible, including on strategic issues, goals and mission.

☆ If your communication enlists and involves your staff, they'll feel a sense of ownership in their work and the company.

☆ Don't ask for employees' opinions if the decision has already been made.

☆ Effective leaders create an 'us' climate.

☆ Hearing and listening are not the same.

☆ Effective active listeners are motivational.

☆ We only hear what we listen for — the rest is just noise.

☆ The left brain listens for logic, facts and data; the right brain for creativity, imagination and emotion.

summary of part three

☆ Always check understanding — the feedback loop helps prevent misunderstanding.

☆ If in doubt — check it out!

☆ Practise productive listening.

11 How the leader impacts the climate

☆ It's good business sense to treat your staff well.

☆ Staff turnover is an invisible profit drain.

☆ Ninety-five percent of your assets drive out the front gate every evening. It's your job to bring them back in the morning.

☆ The leader impacts almost all the reasons people leave their jobs.

☆ People who leave because of poor treatment tend not to tell their employers the real reason.

☆ A positive and productive climate flourishes when people feel valued. It's their perspective that counts, not our intentions.

☆ Inspiring leaders accept unconditionally, help people feel they belong, and build self-worth and feelings of competence in others.

☆ Find out the interests and hobbies of your staff — you may be able to involve them more.

☆ Work out the different intelligences and sensory processing preferences of your staff and you'll find it easier to get good results.

part three: the climate

☆ Don't just tell someone to do a job: instead, ask them how they think it should be done.

☆ Whatever we focus on enlarges.

☆ Praise releases energy — criticism kills it.

☆ Everyone wants credit and recognition for work well done.

☆ 'IQ allows us to think, EQ helps us relate, SQ allows us to do both in times of rapid change.' — Margot Cairnes.

☆ Employees want managers to treat them with respect and courtesy — and not enough managers do.

12 Feedback, criticism and appraisals

☆ Look for opportunities for employees to showcase their talents.

☆ Leaders ensure that accolades are given to their staff, rather than themselves. By doing so they earn huge respect and loyalty from their staff.

☆ Leadership is the art of getting people to do what you want, because they want to.

☆ For effective feedback:

Focus on behaviour and results, not the person.

Praise quickly: correct when appropriate. (It may be just before they do the task the next time.)

Be specific — non-specific comments are a waste of breath.

Take responsibility for your feelings, instead of laying blame.

summary of part three

Don't point the finger — you'll attack their ego.

Use silence — a pause is powerful.

Focus on the behaviour you want, not what you don't want.

☆ Correction:

Start from a positive perspective.

Don't attack their ego.

Give them loopholes.

Don't blame others to make yourself feel more important.

Use the CRC praise sandwich for effective improvement.

Criticise in private.

It's not an exam — supply the answer.

Don't nag — only one criticism to an offence.

Finish any correction on a positive note.

☆ Appraisals:

Ask objective questions, instead of ones that force a 'your opinion versus mine' response.

Review constantly and informally — then it's a breeze.

Get employees to rate themselves first — most of the time they'll be harder on themselves than you would be.

Do appraisals *with* staff, not *to* them — the appraisal is an opportunity for two-way feedback.

13 How to deal with conflict

☆ Complaints are a gift — a chance to correct and improve.

part three: the climate

☆ To deal with angry complaints:

Let them have their say.

Pause before you speak, then use empathy to connect.

Draw them into the solution.

In almost all cases it's not you personally they're unhappy with.

☆ To deal with conflict:

Don't back yourself into a corner — look for a win-win solution.

Don't exaggerate.

Act quickly to correct a problem.

Disagreement and problems handled quickly are only a conversation; left too long, conflict escalates from daily events to challenges to battles.

Fear of conflict freezes us; action releases us.

Many don't address conflict because they don't want to admit it exists.

Decide your goals in relation to the issue.

Work out why it's happening.

Be non-threatening and inclusive in your dialogue.

Anticipate problems and have a Plan B.

Use the 'I' message.

Allow the other person to retreat with dignity.

Be prepared to let a seriously unhappy person go.

Dismissal may be the best and cheapest option, even if they take legal action.

☆ Beware of manipulative people — get rid of them as fast as you can.

summary of part three

14 How to get the message not only delivered but also understood

- ☆ Find out which medium is preferred, if you want to be heard: phone, fax, email, text, written memos or letters.

- ☆ Communication is what is received, not what is sent.

- ☆ Effective leaders express themselves clearly with both the written and spoken word.

- ☆ Poorly written communications imply that the sender either is poorly educated or doesn't care.

- ☆ Write in a crisp, clear, interesting way.

- ☆ Stories bring a document to life.

- ☆ Mark Twain: 'I'm sorry this is such a long letter. I didn't have time for a short one.'

- ☆ Be concise: your message will be more easily understood.

- ☆ Proof, proof, proof.

- ☆ If it's important, proof a hard copy, not on the screen.

part four
the synergy
how to work well together

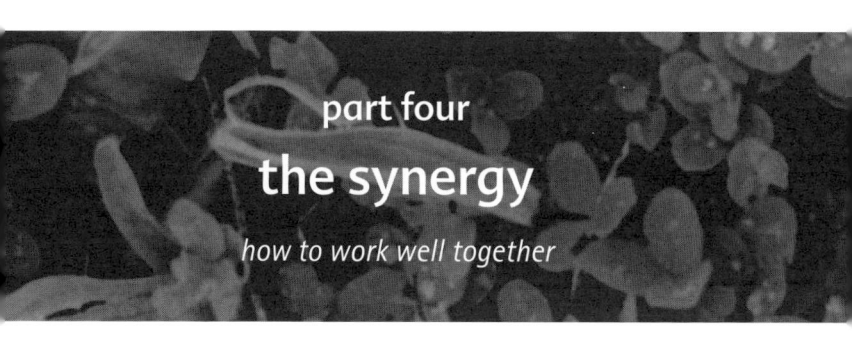

Synergy: the sum of the parts is greater than the individual parts

We've completed three of the four components in the leadership system: foundation, strategy, and climate. We've answered three questions: 'Who are you?', 'Where are you and your organisation going?' and 'What's it like to work here?' The final question is, 'How can we work well together?'

Leaders get people working together effectively for a common goal, for the common good. This is no small task. How do we combine energy and create great results through the efforts of a diverse group of people?

Have you ever watched a magician do party tricks and at the finish you say to the people around you: 'How the heck do they do that stuff? I was watching really closely, but I couldn't see how they did it.'

Observing a really well functioning team is a bit like observing magic — you know something special's going on, but how? And especially if you're suffering the consequences of a less effective team, the bewilderment is sometimes tinged with envy!

Unlike the magic fraternity, we're going to take you behind the scenes to dissect this particular magic. We can't promise you instant success of course — that comes from practice — but when you understand the steps at least you've got somewhere to go, some specific actions and behaviours you can work on.

part four: the synergy

The most exciting and most difficult part of leadership is getting a bunch of independent-thinking people to work effectively together — to create a synergistic unit.

The best leaders create and encourage leaders, not followers. They develop people, support self-leadership, and get results.

15

what are my team's wants, needs and strengths?

In this chapter you'll consider:

☆ How you can get the right people

☆ What makes people tick

☆ What Maslow discovered about people's needs

☆ Generational needs, wants and motivators

Dale Carnegie said: 'The only way I can get you to do anything is by giving you what you want.' Nail that one and you're more than halfway home with a well-functioning team. Learn to work with your people's strengths and you conquer the secret of synergy. Let them work with their strengths, instead of trying to fit square pegs into round holes, and you give them room to shine. Learn to understand them, instead of trying to make everyone agree, and you hold the recipe for successfully functioning teams.

what are my team's wants, needs and strengths?

How can we get the right people?

It's too easy to say, 'Carefully select the right people in your team.' We often don't control the selection. You may be the new boss coming into an established team; someone else may run selection in your organisation; you may be part of a community or political organisation, where people are voted on in a democratic process (and as you look at the line-up you wish for a dictatorship!); or you may have been involved with the selection, done your best, but made a mistake! Hopefully this book will help you manage and lead them.

However, suppose you have the luxury of being involved with the decisions. What do you look for? How do you make the selection? There's a whole industry and science around personnel selection, but let's look at some simple guidelines.

Probably the least accurate method is to get someone you have an instant liking for, especially if you need them to do a job different from your own; the likelihood of achieving the correct combination of skills, personality, attitude and knowledge is pretty slim. Why? Because they're almost always doing different work from you, and a decision based on rapport or empathy is very likely to get the wrong people.

Robyn's story
We needed a new part-time administrator. As soon as the paper hit the streets Sue, an enthusiastic young woman, was on the phone. My retiring administrator and I were so impressed with her apparent skills, CV and attitude we didn't even bother to interview any others, and engaged her with no hesitation. She was very eager — single mother, mature university student, an experienced trainer (although that wasn't part of the job description).

Within 48 hours it was clear we'd made a serious mistake! There

part four: the synergy

was a huge mismatch between the skills Sue had and what the job required. The wasted time just about drove me nuts. It also had a serious impact on my productivity, for as well as training her I still had my normal range of speeches to give and courses to run.

Feeling seriously frustrated and beaten up round the edges, I was indulging in a pity party over drinks a few days later with my friend Christine.

'You should have used a profiling tool,' said Christine. 'You've clearly hired on liking, rather than who's the best for that specific work. You tried to put a square peg in a round hole!'

Within a couple of weeks, to my relief, Sue found she couldn't manage work, study and child, and left, leaving heaps of messy incomplete work.

Within seconds I was on the phone to Christine, whose company uses a DISC profiling tool (one of a number of excellent tools on the market), adapted by Target Training International. (See Resources at back of book.)

'I'm sending you two questionnaires. You score one, not as yourself, but as if you were the job that needs filling. This will highlight the behavioural demands of the job itself — not the behaviour of the person doing the job. Then, when a candidate looks promising, based on their CV and preliminary phone interview, ask them to fill in the other questionnaire. It's similar. It helps them identify their ideal work environment. If there's a reasonable match, only then take the time to interview them and do reference checks. If you need more depth, there's a more comprehensive questionnaire, but for many situations this simple and inexpensive two-pager will do.'

I'd always been slightly disbelieving about the value of these selection tools: however, my 'gut feeling' method had brought terrible results this time, so I was prepared to give it a shot.

The ad was placed and the phone started to ring again. It's very hard to choose when you've got a bunch of equally good-sounding

what are my team's wants, needs and strengths?

people, but I ended up with three who presented very well. Following Christine's instructions, I asked each of them to fill in the questionnaire, before we set a time to meet.

One lady sounded fabulous over the phone and I was really looking forward to meeting her. But Christine came back with: 'Don't go there. You'll waste her time and yours. There's too much of a mismatch. She shows up as needing constant reassurance, but the job shows as needing a lot of independent thinking, an ability to make autonomous decisions without constant reference to you. You know you're out of the office a lot, and travel extensively. If you hire this lady you'll put quite unfair stress on her. She'll be excellent for someone else, but not for you.'

And so I hired Jill, a wonderful office administrator, and just perfect for the job.

Once you're down to the short list, here are some general questions that could be helpful for your interviews. (Tailor them to suit your own situation.) You'll need only about six to get a sense of their working style, the way they handle situations and choices, the way they think.

- Can you tell me about a time, in any job you've done, when you were under a lot of pressure?
- Can you tell me about any incident when you made a mistake on something?
- How did you handle the stress?
- What strategies did you use to overcome it?
- Think back to a time when you were working on an activity requiring a fair degree of detail, and you had deadlines on an important task rapidly approaching. How did you handle it?
- How would you describe your ideal working environment?
- How do you like it to look or feel?

Also consider what you can't live with, and craft questions that hopefully will show up a tendency to that type of behaviour. For instance, Robyn has a strong requirement for tidy work, for staff to put away after themselves, to complete tasks in a timely fashion. An ongoing messy workspace or people who won't put away after themselves frustrates the heck out of her; she *teaches* people how to win the paper war!

So questions relevant to her include: 'Tell me how you'd manage when you've got a number of big tasks to do, deadlines loom, and there's 'stuff' spread around. Do you work around the mess, or tidy up as you go?'

Other tools

As well as DISC, there are a number of other equally effective tools to help: Herrmann Brain Dominance, Myers Briggs, Wilson Learning Styles, Kolbe, Enneagram, Littauer and others. Research in your own marketplace, and if you're filling a senior position in a corporation, you may find it most cost-effective to work with a personnel company.

Just remember, however, these tools and tests are an aid, not the whole process. You must still also use all your normal criteria: common sense and intuition; a good check of the references; and evidence that their previous experience, knowledge and skills will add value to your organisation.

And there's more. Knowledge and skills are important, but not the *most* important quality.

When we look for new staff, we seek a combination of skills, attitude and knowledge. The most important criteria is attitude. Skills and knowledge can be taught, if your candidate has the right attitude. Also take into account the personalities of your existing team. A new person doesn't work in isolation. Will they all work well together? You may even involve other staff in the

what are my team's wants, needs and strengths?

selection, and give the candidate a chance to talk to them without you present.

Never forget — hire in a hurry and you'll repent at leisure.

What makes people tick?

Nearly everyone wants to understand more about the personalities of themselves and those closest to them. The more we understand the characteristics of others the more likely we are, in business and the community, to get the results we want, and at home, to live with happiness rather than discord. Knowledge takes the heat out of potential conflict, and so our time is used more effectively. Instead of spending hours per week trying to mediate, sort out conflict, run continuous damage control, we get on with useful and productive activity. We're free to enjoy life.

Way back into antiquity thinkers in many civilisations dissected character and personality, based on a variety of frameworks — American Indians, ancient Druids, Greeks, Chinese, and others. In AD 160 the Greek philosopher Galen identified four basic 'temperaments' of human nature, how the characteristics could be observed, and how certain behaviour could be predicted according to which temperament you possessed. Most of our modern analysis tools are based on that framework. Almost all are excellent; your preference will often depend on which one you learned first! The key point is not who has the best tool, but what will help you quickly, on the hoof, identify your people's styles, strengths, wants and needs.

To make this discussion really easy, let's link with a very simple tool designed by Des Hunt of Adelaide, Australia, called 'What Makes People Tick?' (But don't be deceived by its simplicity: it's backed by a vast amount of psychology and psychometric testing.) Des uses bird names — Eagle, Peacock, Dove and Owl — to describe the various personalities, and sorts us into the following traits: warm and confident; warm and shy; cool and confident; and cool and shy. You'll be easily able to layer your own favourite tool over the top of this quick overview.

The Eagle

These little charmers are cool and confident. They're strong, dominant personalities, and usually move naturally into leadership positions. Their strength is that they work well without supervision. They don't need a lot of encouragement to perform, but are highly motivated by getting results.

One of their major weaknesses is that they're not very good listeners. They also hate having their time wasted. They tend to snap under stress, then can't understand why others get upset. Others would call them bossy; they call it showing leadership.

If you want to get a favourable response from an Eagle, have your facts straight, get straight to the point, be direct, and for goodness sake, don't nag!

The Peacock

Does someone on your staff like being centre-stage? Do they enjoy fun, parties, noise, and quickly get bored if there's no one else around? They'll almost certainly have a dominant Peacock style, the warm, confident ones of this world. Many salespeople, trainers, motivators and entertainers fit in here. They are great people people, and others (mostly) enjoy being around them. If you've got a job requiring people skills, look for a Peacock.

They're great starters, not such good finishers. Too much detail bores them. (How many sales managers tear their hair out because their salespeople are very sloppy about filling in their

what are my team's wants, needs and strengths?

Figure 21 • What makes people tick?

Style	Eagle	Peacock	Dove	Owl
Basic traits	Cool confident	Warm confident	Warm shy	Cool shy
Other descriptors	Doer Powerful Controller Dominator Enforcer Driver Choleric	Innovator Popular Playful Persuader Promoter Motivator Sanguine	Helper Peaceful Supporter Amiable Phlegmatic	Thinker Perfect Analyser Melancholic
Strengths	Fast High performers Natural leaders Don't need much supervision Confident Decisive Get results Practical	Energetic Inspiring Optimistic Creative Great with people Communicate well Colourful Enjoy centre stage Fun-loving Popular Great initiators	Really helpful Empathetic Supportive Loyal Patient Quiet Good listener Hard worker Go the extra mile	Meticulous Systematic Consistent Thorough Great attention to detail Work well unsupervised
Weaknesses	Poor listeners Intolerant, especially of time wasters Bossy and domineering Undiplomatic Critical Impatient Unbending	Need company Talk too much Poor attention to detail Exaggerate Manipulate Self-centred Noisy Undisciplined Easily bored	Easily led Indecisive Dependent Need other people Stubborn Not good initiators Don't like speaking out in public Easily overlooked Sensitive Struggle to say no	Introverted Shy Poor socialisers Indecisive Critical Self-righteous Inflexible Over-cautious Often feel inadequate Pessimist
Seen by others as	Pushy Uncaring Tough Dominating Bossy Short-sighted Status-seeking	Unrealistic Impractical Scattered Fanatic Excitable Disorganised Out of touch Loud Over the top	Over-sensitive Possessive Conforming Postponing Over-personalising Indecisive Not serious Boring Push-over	Perfectionist Rigid Unemotional Too critical Picky Indecisive Over-serious Boring Too quiet

Continued

part four: the synergy

Style	Eagle	Peacock	Dove	Owl
Needs	Results Challenge Action The chance to lead and make decisions Succinct facts	To be noticed Popularity Applause & praise Status symbols Recognition Appreciation Others around them	Acceptance Belonging Friendship Harmony Peace To be important to the team	Procedures Rules Guidelines Time to get it right Quiet Systems
Motivators	Winning Prestige Position and titles Freedom from supervision, controls & detail Power to achieve results Chance for rapid advancement	Popularity and social recognition Freedom of speech and people to talk to Freedom from control and detail New adventures Fun and excitement	Involvement Status quo Sincerity Recognition for dedication	Progress Quality Reassurance that they're doing a good job Limited exposure – they like working alone Personal attention
How to motivate	Support their goals Identify cost Be concise Explain logic Give broad issues first, and only enough detail to make fast decisions Focus on results Don't waste their time	Support their ideas Explain long-term effect Offer fun ideas first Be expressive with voice and body Focus on effectiveness Give plenty of praise and interaction with others	Support their feelings Show impact on people Present points of agreement first Support ideas with experience Focus on teamwork Show appreciation Don't take for granted	Support their work Be logical first Present details as well as the big picture Show the practical and realistic side Focus on quality Give them plenty of time
Favourite sayings	It's my way or the highway! Get out of my way Next!	Look at me! Didn't I do well!	How can I help? What do you want? Are you OK?	Let me check that I'll have to think about it I'm not sure
To be more effective	Tone down Be more considerate	Keep calendar Follow up details Moderate loudness	Be more assertive Don't take on work that others should do Learn to say no	Be less critical Avoid unnecessary perfectionism

what are my team's wants, needs and strengths?

paperwork accurately?) Quieter souls think they are much too loud and pushy; they think the quiet ones are boring!

To get the best out of Peacocks you must be prepared to encourage and praise them. They thrive on it. They are energised by being around others, and stressed by being on their own for too long. Don't put them in a lonely work environment; they won't be able to perform effectively. They need to know that they are appreciated, and even when they know they've done a good job, they still like to be told.

The Dove

If we didn't have the peace-loving, supportive Doves, life would be pretty uncomfortable. These folk are the salt of the earth. They are warm, shy types. They enjoy being around other people, as long as they don't have to take centre stage. They really enjoy being support people. If you want someone to do something, chances are it is almost always a Dove who offers. They make great listeners and sympathisers. You'll find them in helping roles such as nurses, counsellors and support positions. They are happiest when people need them. If the people around them are unhappy, they are unhappy.

Don't expect them to initiate things, though. That's way outside their comfort zone. They prefer not to speak out in public meetings. It is very easy to crush a Dove and not even realise it, for they find it very uncomfortable to stand up for themselves. Therefore managers have to be more thoughtful for their Doves than their more vocal staff.

Doves are the kind-hearted souls who'll sacrifice their own needs for the last-minuting Peacock, or the domineering Eagle who comes rushing in demanding something, without checking what else the Dove has to do. These are the ones who have the hardest job to say no to unreasonable demands.

part four: the synergy

The Owl

You always knew owls were wise birds, didn't you! So are human Owls. Here we have the cool, shy folk of society. They make great accountants, lawyers, researchers or anyone who needs high accuracy in their work. They thrive on being right. In fact, the possibility of having to pass work in without being able to check it several times is just about enough to bring on an anxiety attack. Their strength is their attention to detail.

Their weakness is they find it very hard to make a quick decision. Don't expect an Owl to make a quick decision — what if it was wrong!

The best way to get good results out of Owls is to give them plenty of time to do a good, well-checked job. Don't expect them to be happy about a rushed job, and don't expect them to enjoy making quick decisions. Give them a good briefing. Also, don't expect them to be happy in a work environment where they have to do heaps of interacting. They prefer a 'smattering of shush', so they can get on and do their job well.

We have found that most companies have a predominance of Doves and Owls, which is probably just as well. You know the old saying of 'too many Chiefs and not enough Indians' don't you? And fancy having a whole company of Peacocks. There'd never be any work done — they'd all be too busy chatting and having a good time!

What Maslow discovered about people's needs

Some research just hits the spot. Back in 1935, Abraham Maslow came up with a theory still taught and respected today: the Hierarchy of Needs.

He identified that all individuals have five core needs that can be arranged in a hierarchy from the most basic to the

what are my team's wants, needs and strengths?

highest level; that as each need was satisfied it was replaced with another. He also taught that we *cannot* move up to the next level unless our present needs are met. This means that a need is a motivator, and once it's satisfied it no longer motivates. What a great clue that is for you as a leader, trying to motivate your troops!

☆ *Level 1* Physiological needs: food, water, shelter, sex, and the ability to care for our children.

☆ *Level 2* Safety needs: At this level the person is concerned about security and protection. This translates most directly into concerns for short-term and long-term job security, as well as physical safety on the job.

☆ *Level 3* Social needs: These are satisfied through social acceptance and group membership, as well as the need to receive love, affection and belonging.

☆ *Level 4* Esteem needs: These relate to our desire to achieve, hold prestigious positions, receive recognition and appreciation, shine in our work. Satisfaction of esteem needs leads to feelings of self-confidence, worth and usefulness. Failure to satisfy esteem needs leads to feelings of failure and inadequacy.

☆ *Level 5* Self-actualisation: These needs reflect an individual's desire to grow and develop to the fullest potential. An individual often wants the opportunity to be creative on the job or desires autonomy, responsibility and challenge.

part four: the synergy

Figure 22 • Maslow's Hierarchy of Needs

```
           Level 5
       Self-actualisation
          Level 4
        Esteem needs
          Level 3
        Social needs
          Level 2
        Safety needs
          Level 1
      Physiological needs
```

Many of us change levels as we step in and out of different life roles. At work we may be at Level 5, self-actualisation, but as a partner we may be at Level 3, social needs, seeking affection and belonging.

Once you've mastered a level, it doesn't mean you will stay at that level. We move down the pyramid faster than up. A sales manager was removed from his job with little notice. He zoomed from Level 4: esteem needs to Level 1: physiological needs, worried he'd be unable to buy groceries or make the house payment.

Generational needs, wants and motivators

As well as personality styles and the core life needs identified by Maslow, we've also got generational needs and wants. As people's lifespans and working lives have extended, we often find four generations in a workplace. Helping them bridge the gaps is essential for creating synergy in your workplace.

what are my team's wants, needs and strengths?

Traditionals (1922—43)
This generation saw or felt the hard times of the Great Depression. Most grew up in homes with stay-at-home mothers and two parents. They learned hard work, conformity, law and order and loyalty at an early age. They respect authority and do what they're asked to do. They're not apt to disagree with authority figures. They bring the value of what has and hasn't worked in the past.

Wants: They want to do a good job. They want to be told what to do.

Motivators: They're motivated by money and a respect for their experience. As their leader, show that you value their loyalty and the fact that they take pride in doing their work well.

Baby Boomers (1943—60)
This generation experienced post-war prosperity, television, the space race and women's liberation. Most also grew up in homes with stay-at-home mothers and two parents. They value optimism, work, involvement, teams, and health and wellness. They want to make a difference and are willing to do whatever it takes. They're willing to come in early and work late.

Wants: They want to be asked for their ideas. They want input into decisions. They want to know as much as they can about the organisation.

Motivators: Baby boomers are motivated by making a difference, being involved, knowing they are important to the organisation's success. They usually like to feel needed.

Generation X (1960—80)
This generation were latchkey kids, many from single-parent

part four: the synergy

homes. They grew up with MTV, Aids, and computers. They value family, diversity, techno-literacy, and leisure. They grew up in daycare centres — peers are important. They value social connections and fun at work. They are not intimidated by authority and dislike meetings and politics. They are creative, adaptable and self-reliant.

Wants: They like managers who make decisions and move on. They want to know the expected outcome and then be left to achieve it. They want to know how to access information and the people they need.

Motivators: Generation Xers are motivated by autonomy, the newest hardware and software, an informal work environment, and flexible or reduced work hours. (Let them choose the hours.) They like to balance work with the rest of family life, and they enjoy the feeling of being on the fast track.

Other things that motivate Generation Xers include:

☆ Work environments with childcare centre, on-site dry-cleaning, ATMs, fabulous cafeteria food including dinners-to-go, athletic facilities.

☆ Fair, competent leaders.

☆ Fun.

☆ Casual, educational, non-micro-managed work climate.

☆ Frequent feedback about work (not just an annual performance appraisal).

☆ Immediate reward.

☆ Virtual teamwork.

☆ Perks like golf membership, gift certificates.

what are my team's wants, needs and strengths?

☆ Clear goals.

☆ Opportunities to learn new things.

☆ Training that makes them more marketable.

☆ Knowing how their job fits into the whole picture.

☆ Action.

☆ Ownership of new projects — to be clear on results expected.

☆ Time with the boss — they want to know what you know.

Net Generation (1980—2000)

This generation grew up with computers, TV talk shows and multiculturalism. They are optimistic, confident and street smart. They value civic duty and morality. They trust and value the traditional generation. They are the best-educated generation and have multi-tasking ability.

Wants: They want supervision and structure. They may be intimidated by difficult people and, if so, will need support.

Motivators: The Net Generation are motivated by working with other bright, creative people, being a hero, helping turn companies around, the opportunity to work with strong, ethical leaders, mentoring programmes, generous rewards, recognition and praise.

(Source: *The Futurist*, March/April 2000. 'Know the difference between the four generations — work from wants'.)

part four: the synergy

Leadership lessons

- ☑ 'The only way I can get you to do anything is by giving you what you want.' — Dale Carnegie.

- ☑ Use profiling tools to get the right staff — empathy and liking will tend to get you someone like yourself.

- ☑ Hire in a hurry and repent at leisure.

- ☑ Understand what makes your people tick and you'll get the results you want, instead of running perpetual damage control.

- ☑ Maslow's Hierarchy of Needs shows us five levels of need. A need is a motivator: once it is satisfied it no longer motivates.

- ☑ Different generations are motivated by different things.

16

how do I get the best out of them?

In this chapter you'll consider:

☆ Leading from the front

☆ Focus and clarity — know where you're heading and what your key objectives are

☆ Quick and effective decision-making

☆ Self and time management

☆ How to run effective meetings

☆ Delegation

Lead from the front

Set a good example of the behaviour you want them to model. So simple, and yet too many managers don't do it! If you want to lead, get into the trenches. We've all seen movies and heard jokes and stories about leaders whose leadership style is 'do as I say, not as I do'. The ones whose workers respect them and are willing to go the extra mile, don't fit that stereotype.

part four: the synergy

Macedonian warrior emperor Alexander the Great is possibly the greatest military strategist, tactician and ruler in world history; military, political and business leaders around the world have studied his principles of leadership for centuries. When he died of sickness (possibly malaria) on 11 June in 323 BC, at the age of 32, he had conquered almost all the known world. His empire stretched from the Balkans in central Europe down to southern Europe, and from northern Africa through all of Asia up to northwest India. As his army rolled unstoppably on he conquered several great ancient empires and civilisations: Persia (which had ruled much of Asia for over three centuries), Egypt, Babylon, Assyria and India.

There were many factors that made Alexander great, including his teacher, Aristotle. He was a brilliant motivator, strategist and thinker. One of his key attributes was that he was always in the thick of the fight, the hottest part of the battle — and he never asked of his troops what he wouldn't do himself.

General Sir Edmund Allenby in the First World War and Lieutenant General Bernard Montgomery ('Monty') in the Second World War led victories in the Middle East that played major parts in the ultimate Allied victories. They each took over from less effective commanders who had lost numerous battles on their critically important battle fronts. Allenby's and Monty's soldiers loved and respected them; just like Alexander they asked nothing of their men they wouldn't do themselves. For instance, both of them moved their headquarters out of the comfort of Cairo's hotels, from where their predecessors had commanded, to the desert, living rough alongside their men. The message very quickly filtered through; any officers who wanted to make an impression got out of their comfortable soft beds and joined them on the hot, thirsty, dangerous front.

A young officer heard some of his soldiers grumbling about digging

how do I get the best out of them?

latrines at the end of a day's march. He said nothing. Instead, he took off his jacket, grabbed a spade and stepped down into the trench. Spade turned; dirt flew. Twenty minutes later, he passed the spade to one of the now silent complainers who, shamefaced, got on with his job. Over time he found that soldiers regularly asked to be transferred to his unit. His reputation was 'hard but fair'.

Most of us are not in military situations, but at times work situations feel like a battle zone to the participants. A true leader leads by example.

Focus and clarity

Leaders get buy-in from the team by having a clear vision of where they're going ... and a passion for getting there. Employees are anchored; goals are tied to mission and vision, job description and to performance appraisal. Employees give leaders their short-term goals; leaders give employees long-term goals. Leaders also bridge the gap between employee goals, manager goals and organisation goals.

How to demonstrate focus and clarity

Be clear as to your expectations. Clearly articulate purpose, vision and goals. In Chapter 1, in the example of the new president of a voluntary organisation, everyone kept a clear focus of the mission of the organisation, and so disagreements were easily defused and positive action followed.

High expectations equals better performance. Be the one who believes in your team's ability to perform with greatness before they believe it themselves. Magic happens when someone believes in us.

part four: the synergy

Dan Jansen, a famous American speed skating champion, completed three Olympics in a row before he won a gold medal in the 1994 Olympic Winter Games in Lillehammer. Although Dan was a brilliant sprinter, every time he stopped short of winning.

He had grown up on the ice with his friend Bonnie Blair, the most decorated American Winter Olympics athlete, as well as record holder for the most gold medals (five) won by an American woman in any sport. Until 1994 Dan's view was, 'Bonnie's successful, I'm not.'

Bonnie believed in him. His family believed in him. His nation believed in him. Finally he got out of his own way, worked on his mental state, and learned to believe in himself. That Olympics his fans watched in awe as he won the 1000-metres gold medal, which was not his best event. Dan set a new world record, the fastest in history.

The magic of belief is a powerful force. When someone believes in you, you begin to believe in yourself. Dan Jansen proved that believing in ourselves changes history.

And don't just believe in your people — communicate it positively.

Decision-making — how to cut to the chase

Good leaders don't vacillate: they make decisions quickly. They're not always right, but at least they do make them. Eighty percent of all decisions should be made now! Many times it doesn't matter what the decision is, as long as one is made. Insistence on having all the facts first can dramatically slow up results. No one deliberately seeks mistakes, but if they happen, accept them as part of the learning process. Accept risks as inevitable, within the parameters of common sense.

If you find it hard to make quick decisions, maybe you're high in Owl or Analyser traits. These types need all the data before they feel comfortable; they double-check every detail before they can recommend any course of action. They hate being wrong, or even *possibly* wrong. But there's a Chinese proverb that says, 'He who deliberates fully before taking a step will spend entire life on one leg.'

If you are an Owl, learn to listen to your intuition, which may be described as the instantaneous application of past experience (and is becoming more and more recognised as a legitimate business tool). Practise quick decision-making in small things, like what meal to have at a restaurant. You might get to like it eventually!

If you haven't got good fact-finding processes, institute some. Maybe put the subject on a staff meeting agenda, and listen to what your staff say.

Tips to improve your decision-making process
Improve fact-finding procedures
Most indecision is caused by ignorance, fear, or lack of confidence in the facts. Improve your fact-finding procedures, and learn to listen to your intuition. Use the following questions to clear your thinking:

- What result do we want?
- What benefits are there in each of the possible options?
- What can go wrong?
- What other ways are there of achieving the same result?
- What other information do I need before I can make this decision?
- Who do I need to speak to in order to get that information?
- What is my gut instinct here?

Still confused? A very easy way to get clarity is to create a plus and minus balance sheet. In the sales world it's sometimes

part four: the synergy

called a Franklin Close, and is used to help a reluctant purchaser make a decision. Once you've got your confused and jumbled thoughts on paper it's usually obvious which path to take.

Figure 23 • Franklin Close technique

Example: Should I take on a new staff member in Marketing?

PROS	Score 5 (high) → 1 (low)	*CONS*	Score 5 (high) → 1 (low)
It will relieve the pressure in the marketing department	4	We'll have to adjust the budget to compensate for an extra salary	4
Sally is threatening to leave, because she can't manage the workload.	3	We'll have to move the partitions around to seat someone else.	1
We'll keep a good staff member.	5	Time is needed to integrate and train a new staff member onto the team.	5
We'll have enough resources to run the new campaign internally, instead of having to outsource it.	5		
If we don't employ someone else now it will be much harder to train someone else when we hit our busy season.	3		
TOTAL	20	TOTAL	10

Conclusion: There's no time like the present. The advantages outweigh the disadvantages.

Note: Let weight, not quantity, determine your decision.

how do I get the best out of them?

Consider your group decision-making style

Good leaders make decisions that are in the best interests of the whole organisation. Since people often resist change when they don't participate in the 'decision-making' process it's important to consider what group decision-making style you use most often. Is it *command, consultative,* or *consensus?*

☆ Command
Command decision-making is deciding without asking for suggestions or ideas from outside sources. The advantage is fast decisions and you make the decision. This style is good in emergency situations but if overused team morale and effort will suffer.

☆ Consultative
Consultative decision-making is deciding after asking others for ideas, suggestions, knowledge or information. This is slower, because you have to wait for others' input. Since the team is involved, there is less surprise for people. However, the team needs to understand you will make the final decision. Their role is input. To avoid unnecessary delays, you could send an invitation for input, and say, 'If I haven't heard from you by … [time], this is what I'll do.'

☆ Consensus
Consensus decision-making is deciding after everyone agrees and buys in on the decision. This is time-consuming, as the group makes the decision. The benefit is teamwork, security and a higher probability of success because of the many ideas, skills and perspectives involved.

Never ask for the opinion of others when your mind is already made up.

part four: the synergy

Use lateral-thinking techniques

Sometimes a creative approach will jog your thinking in unexpected and useful ways. The 'father' of lateral thinking is Edward de Bono, with his *Six Thinking Hats* method (and he's written many other books on creative thinking). It gives a very clear way to clarify your thoughts on any issue. You mentally put on one coloured hat at a time, and consider the question under review only from that perspective. Then move on to another colour. You may not pass on to another style of thinking until you've gone as far as you can with the hat in use.

White Hat	Information	What are the facts?
Red Hat	Feelings	What do I feel about this?
Black Hat	Judgement	What is wrong with this?
Yellow Hat	Benefits	What are the good points?
Blue Hat	Thinking	What thinking is needed?
Green Hat	Creativity	What new ideas are possible?

The process of focused consideration clears the brain, and helps us see the real issues. It cuts through the mental traffic jams. The benefits of this kind of process are that it:

☆ Moves the team from adversarial to cooperative thinking.

☆ Reduces meeting times by up to 70 percent.

☆ Removes the politics that often bedevil a decision-making meeting.

☆ Provides a different yet common language for decision-making.

☆ Gets faster results.

how do I get the best out of them?

There are now many books and courses dealing with creative thinking. Ask around in your community, and check the search engines. We've also listed a few others in the bibliography.

Self and time management

Effective prioritising is a major time challenge for most people, and yet it is a simple skill to master. Here are ten tips for effective time management

1: Write down your goals

When you write down your goals it becomes easier to know where your priorities lie. You can then, with greater ease, stay focused when seductive time stealers try to lure you away.

2: Develop a proactive focus

Become forward focused, anticipate deadlines and act before they arrive. Also, constantly seek for better ways to do things. Not only will you remove a vast amount of stress, but you'll also feel much more in control of events.

3: Learn to say no

If you can politely say no when asked to invest time into activities that don't match your goals, you consistently achieve more. Listen to your intuition; it will guide you.

4: Put aside 'red' time

Many workplaces are open plan, with constant interruptions between the staff. Many managers think managing means being available at all times for their staff. Result? People either go home frustrated because they haven't been able to get their real work done, or work longer hours to try and catch up. Solution:

shut doors, use quiet rooms, divert the phone, do not allow interruptions, for at least one hour a day.

5: Don't major in minor things

Many folk try to get the little things handled before they start on their big tasks. The outcome? The important tasks pile up, and they get bogged down in minutiae and perfectionism. Instead, handle the things that really matter first. You'll be amazed at how the small activities fit in and around the important activities.

6: Do it NOW

Instead of *thinking* about what you'd like to do, get started. Create momentum, make the first move, and the rest will follow. Try putting the following quotation on your bathroom wall: 'If I do today what others won't, I'll have tomorrow what others can't.'

7: Don't squeeze in tasks

Are you a last minuter, often arriving stressed and flustered at your destination? Remember that 'one last thing' you squeezed in before you left, thinking you were being efficient — don't do it! Some people are naturally punctual; others struggle. It's all to do with the way we process time. The strugglers who try to squeeze in yet another task, as they head out the door, almost always get an intuitive nudge not to do it, but push that thought away. Listen!

8: In order to go faster, first you must go slower

New tasks and better ways to do things take time to learn and internalise. Expect to be a little slower at first, and take the time to learn the best methods you can. The initial slowness is rapidly recouped, and the time saved is long term.

9: Do it better
Always look for ways to shorten and improve each activity. Hold a permanent question in your mind: 'How can I improve this activity?' The danger is that we fall into a comfort zone, and don't want to change. Welcome the opportunity to change and improve.

10: Eliminate clutter
Messy desk, office, house, bedroom, office, garage, car — it doesn't matter what it is. When things are lying around, your subconscious mind has to work harder to ignore the 'mind traffic' distractions: you become slower and less effective. Do yourself a favour and clear up as you go. The feeling of freedom is its own reward.

Run effective meetings
Achieving effective meetings is a major challenge for most people. Most of us learn how to run meetings by attending them, which is often not a good model. Before you call a meeting, ask yourself:

☆ What is the purpose of the meeting?

☆ Is it related to my overall goals?

☆ What do I expect from the participants?

☆ Is it *really* needed, or could we achieve a result in a quicker way?

Meeting process
If a meeting is the best answer, use the following easy process to help you.

part four: the synergy

- *Before the meeting*
  Plan the meeting carefully: who, what, where, when, why, how many
  Prepare and send out the agenda days in advance
  Come early and set up the meeting room

- *At the beginning of the meeting*
  Greet and mingle
  Start on time
  Use an ice-breaker opening
  Re-establish the agenda and finish time

- *During the meeting*
  Redirect when people stray from agenda
  Focus, clarify vague input, summarise
  Follow parliamentary procedure for motions

  Steps to handle motions
  1. A member is recognised by the Chair
  2. A motion is made
  3. The motion is seconded
  4. The Chair states the motion to the Committee
  5. The motion is discussed
  6. The Chair repeats the motion and puts it to a vote
  7. The Chair states the results: 'Motion carried/defeated'

- *Before adjournment*
  Identify action items: who, what, when
  Set date, place of next meeting (develop preliminary agenda)
  Close meeting on a positive note
  Clean room

- *Following adjournment*
  Mail minutes within 48 hours!

Chairperson's roles

The chairperson's key role is tracking, including and confronting: it's not a privileged soapbox.

Tracking

You are in charge of process. Help members focus by selecting a timekeeper to monitor time. Appoint someone to take minutes. Make minutes useful: short, punchy action points, distributed soon after the meeting is over. Make use of action plans as a communication and tracking tool for follow-up work.

Including

You are responsible for the climate. Help people feel cohesive and comfortable. As the meeting progresses, hear from each person at the meeting. We no longer have the luxury of simply belonging — if people have nothing to contribute, they shouldn't be there. Ask the quiet members for their thoughts or feelings. End the meeting with a round robin asking something like 'Do you have anything more before we adjourn?'

Confronting

You are responsible for confronting bad behaviour. Author and consultant Sister Mary Bennet McKinney says, 'Confront the person who never stops talking; confront the person who never starts talking; confront the person who has temper tantrums; confront the person who uses silence to manipulate. At least 80 percent of the people who malfunction in a group think they are helping.'

Extra meetings tips

- You *can* be on time for meetings! Block out 15 minutes either side as soon as you accept.

part four: the synergy

- Don't wait for latecomers, start without them or leave — even when it's the boss.
- Make it 'our' meeting by assigning team members to present agenda items.
- Send any relevant printed material before the meeting, preferably with the agenda.
- Don't allow phones in the room.
- Don't let a meeting go more than an hour without a break. People's attention span is dictated by what happens in the lower part of their anatomy.
- Suggest the team set ground rules to address behaviour (such as: no side-conversations) and expectations (such as: all meetings begin on time). This will save confronting later.
- Consider new technology in meetings, like teleconferences or conference calls. The upside is this saves time, reduces expense and focuses conversation; the downside is that it's less personal, there's a risk of incomplete communication, and sometimes technical difficulties.

Example of agenda
(Time, Date, Location)

10.00 am	1.	Ice breaker and Call to Order
10.05 am	2.	Additions, Corrections, Approval of Minutes
10.10 am	3.	Committee Reports
10.30 am	4.	Old Business
10.50 am	5.	New Business
11.00 am	6.	Summary and Adjournment

Some useful 'filtering' questions for meetings

If you are asked to attend a meeting, consider the following before you accept:

- Do I really need to be there?
- If you need input from our department, can someone else attend instead of me?
- Are decisions likely to be made that only I can make, or can I delegate or sidestep?
- For which part of the agenda will you need my input?
- I may need to leave after my contribution. What time will you be dealing with the topics related to me?

Delegation

One of the hardest things for many managers to do is get out of the way and let their people get on with the job! Non-mastery of this core skill will keep you shovelling coal while others enjoy the scenery on the wonderful journey of leadership. The problem is that very few have formal training in it. Many lurch along, doing their best, often overwhelmed by their own work as well as the needs of their people and trying not to feel resentful at the time it takes to train others.

However, master this skill and you move into a different league: the exciting world of new horizons. You're free of the tasks that others at a lower pay rate, lesser skill set, or fewer responsibilities can do as well as you. It is a high-performance leadership style that produces long-term results.

Good delegators give their subordinates as much responsibility and authority as they are able to accept but at the same time maintain control. Paradoxically, good delegators increase their own power by sharing it with others. And communication is key. A Harvard management specialist, after much research, came to the conclusion that all good managers know intuitively — that the ability to communicate clear expectations was a manager's most important leadership and motivational tool.

A common problem for would-be delegators is that they don't realise delegation is a four-stage train journey, not a one-stop destination. If you don't step through each phase with the person you're delegating to, at some point along the line you'll almost certainly have to backtrack. Master these four steps, learn to be patient in the initial stages, and you'll achieve better results faster. Yes, you could have done the job faster — at the beginning. But that's a sure path to limiting your growth and success. Once you've trained someone up properly you're free to move on to new challenges and opportunities.

The four stages of delegation

1: Directive behaviour by the delegator — High Direction, Low Support

Initially a new person needs instruction, not the opportunity to use their initiative. You'll give them lots of directions, and only a low amount of support in making decisions. They don't yet know enough to need much support.

2: Coaching behaviour by the delegator — High Direction, High Support

They are starting to understand the process. You encourage them to come with questions; you give plenty of explanations, continue to instruct, and also support them in learning and applying new skills and knowledge.

3: Supportive behaviour by the delegator — Low Direction, High Support
These folks are getting a good grip on the process. You're weaning both yourself and them off lots of 'telling'. You now support them in making the decisions. Your role is to help where needed, review their actions and oversee results as they increase their level of responsibility.

4: Delegating behaviour by the delegator — Low Direction, Low Support
Now you're free. Your delegatee not only has an excellent understanding of the task, but they have the confidence to get on with the job. They can still come for help if they need it, but that's a rare occurrence.

(This thinking is expanded in Kenneth Blanchard's excellent little book *Leadership and the One Minute Manager.*)

Further tips for great delegation

Getting started with delegation
Find an area in each project that can be given away. There's almost always some part that can be farmed out, even if it's only small.

Paint the big picture
Once people understand the task, let them get on with it — they may have a better way. The most important point to communicate is the desired outcome. Show people how their efforts will contribute to the overall result. Much poor work from employees is caused by confusion because of unclear explanations. We all operate better when we know what we're doing. Remember always: once someone is trained, managers should direct what needs to be done, not how it's done.

part four: the synergy

Deadlines
Set sensible deadlines together, communicate them clearly, and teach the staff member to use a results chart for tracking (see the end of Part Two on strategic planning). Allow cushions of time so that if something goes wrong you still have time to correct.

Review times
If checkpoints are established before commencement, and the employee knows about them, it becomes a learning process for them, not a negative correction.

Accountability
When you ask for something to be done by a specified date, let the person concerned see you write it in your planner. It keeps them accountable.

Questions to check understanding
Avoid that killer question: 'Do you understand?' It almost always gets a 'yes', because no one wants to look silly. Instead, use open-ended questions such as:

- ☆ 'I'm bound to have overlooked some details. What would you like me to go over again?'

- ☆ 'You'll have some questions, I'm sure. What would you like to check on?'

- ☆ 'I know that's a lot of information to take in at once. Go away, have a think about it and come back in [*and name a time that's convenient for you*] with how you'll go about it, and any further questions.'

- ☆ 'So where do you think is the best way to start?'

☆ 'What ideas spring to mind, or points would you like to discuss further?'

Teaching the delegatee to think

Avoid 'reverse delegation'. Once a person has a good grasp on a task, don't let them interrupt you with a question unless they also bring two possible solutions. It forces them to think more, and you'll be saved many unnecessary interruptions.

Make yourself redundant (at least in part)

A good manager looks constantly for ways to make themselves redundant. Be prepared to delegate challenging jobs, as well as boring ones. When you give someone else the chance to learn your job, it frees you to move on to better things. If you operate from a fear that someone else may take over your position, that is what you will attract towards yourself. On the other hand, if you help someone below you to be as good as yourself, you create the opportunity for further advancement for yourself.

Remember that like attracts like. If you are generous in helping other people to advance, and operate from a generous spirit, you will attract generosity in return.

However, resist promoting poor people managers to senior jobs, especially those who have a poor record of keeping people for whom they have line-management responsibilities.

Praise

(Already discussed in Chapter 11, but no section on delegation can omit it!)

Remember, praise releases energy, criticism kills it. Don't worry too much about what's not right — praise to the goal. Constant focus on what they've done wrong will only increase tension and mistakes and you won't achieve your goal for improvement. Also, allow others the opportunity to shine and don't hog the credit. This builds team spirit and a sense of importance for the colleague concerned. If someone is actively involved in a project, and honoured for that involvement, they enjoy greater work satisfaction.

Some folk need coaxing
Not everyone thinks they can handle more work. Sometimes you have to actively encourage people to take more responsibility. They may have to be constantly reinforced in the rightness of their decisions. People who won't take responsibility are either lazy or need gentle encouragement. Sometimes the best solution is just to drop them in at the deep end and make them answerable for their actions (but only do that when you're quite sure they've been trained properly, can do the task, and you can live with the consequences if there's a mistake).

Can this person manage?
Don't overload the willing horse. If you are going to give a bigger than usual task to an employee, prepare them well in advance so they don't feel overwhelmed.

What's the risk?
Evaluate the risk of delegating. Ask yourself 'What is the worst possible thing that can happen if I pass this job on?' If the consequences are severe, either don't delegate, or establish very regular checkpoints.

To study time management, effective meetings or delegation in more depth, Robyn's best-sellers, *Getting a Grip on Time* and *About Time — 120 Tips for Those with No Time*, are a very easy

how do I get the best out of them?

practical source. Further information on all her products can be found at http://www.gettingagripontime.com.

Leadership lessons

- ☑ If you want to lead, get into the trenches.
- ☑ A great leader provides focus and clarity.
- ☑ Good leaders are fast decision-makers.
- ☑ Practise lateral (or creative) thinking.
- ☑ Become an excellent manager of your time choices.
- ☑ Run effective meetings — short, sharp, focused and to the point.
- ☑ Good delegators increase their own power by sharing it with others.
- ☑ Delegation is a four-stage train ride, not a one-step destination.
- ☑ Look for ways to make yourself redundant.
- ☑ Don't put focus on what's wrong; praise to the goal.

17

into the future

leaders who can lead through change

In this chapter you'll consider:

- ☆ Change — good or bad? How to surf the waves of change, and still stay standing!
- ☆ How to manage information overwhelm
- ☆ Clones, offspring or successors? How to replicate yourself through the four stages of team development

How can you develop people and get results, while everything keeps changing? Employees and managers are in the same foxhole, struggling to follow the same ground rules for working in speed-of-light change. Good leaders know they have to lead themselves through change before they can lead others, so let's finish this book with some useful change strategies. Then we'll wrap up with some ideas on how to encourage future leaders, how to develop your people.

into the future

Change — too much, too fast?

In 1970 Alvin Toffler described the symptoms of a new disease he called 'future shock'. He saw it as a psycho-biological condition caused by exposing people to 'too much change in too short a time'. Toffler argued that technological and social changes were happening so rapidly that people could no longer adapt to them. He said: 'Unless mankind quickly learns to control the rate of change in their personal affairs as well as in society at large, we are doomed to a massive adaptational breakdown'.

Today, only a few decades since Toffler wrote that much-quoted book, change has become a way of life. The business climate moves and changes incredibly fast. Technology has wiped out traditional boundaries; many of us work globally, with parts of our work outsourced to companies located on the other side of the world. Many sell some or all their products or services offshore; more and more people tele-commute from their homes to an office which could be 30 minutes away, or a 22-hour plane ride away. It's a time of exciting opportunity, and for those who don't like such rapid change, a time of overwhelming uncertainty.

However, the *speed* of change has caught us unaware, despite Toffler's warnings. For too many, day-to-day work consumes us. Busy, busy, busy is the chant; too busy to look ahead; too busy to plan for succession; too busy to mentor; too busy to care for ourselves. People in workplaces all over the world cry: 'Is this all there is?' With this frenetic pace, we're in danger of meaning and passion in our lives being sucked away while we struggle for air.

As Toffler warned, some people have suffered severe stress with this overwhelming change. But it's not all doom and gloom: there are solutions, and plenty of folk cope very well indeed. People can adapt — after all, the human race exists because we're masters at survival! There are exciting new skills to learn, exciting new frontiers to explore. The business of learning to manage change enables us to enjoy happy, fulfilled and productive lives in this web-speed world, and still stay sane!

We can break the subject into three areas.

1 *Process:* Understand the process of change, and what's happening.

2 *Pitfalls:* Avoid three common pitfalls that hinder successful acceptance of change.

3 *New skills:* Expand our survival strategies to deal with change.

1: The process of change

Think about a change in your own life, good or bad. A new job, baby, new home, major loss, a life-threatening illness, family members in dangerous situations, work pressure ...

Life is a cycle of transitions. Many of the items listed above are a normal part of life. However, combined with the speed of the Internet, the increasing speed of information flow, the speed with which changes occur in business, those natural transitions compound the sense of being overwhelmed and subsequent stress felt by so many people in business today. Let's look briefly at two ways of analysing, simplifying and understanding this process, for when you chunk out an issue into small components it never seems as complex.

The four stages of change
Elisabeth Kubler-Ross has broken our response to change into four stages — all normal. And they operate on little day-to-day

events as well as large, life-changing ones. Think of the last time you got frustrated with your computer because it chose to have a bad-hair day! These stages are:

1. *Denial:* We rationalise, look back at the good old days and refuse to hear new information.

2. *Resistance:* We feel angry and frustrated. We blame others, we complain, and then we begin to doubt our ability.

3. *Exploration:* As we begin to adjust to the change, we begin to explore. We may have trouble with focus and decision-making, but slowly we expand our vision, look for answers and begin to see new possibilities.

4. *Commitment:* Finally, we become committed to the change. We cooperate, find balance, participate in teamwork and feel focused again.

Transitions

Now let's put another layer on this process — similar to Kubler-Ross but different enough to spend a minute on. William Bridges talks about change in a different way. In his book *Transitions*, he defines change as an external outcome and transitions as an internal process that individuals go through. These transitions he sees as Letting Go, the Neutral Zone and New Beginnings.

- *Letting Go — the beginning of change*

Before change can occur, we have to let go of what was. Letting go faster is a way to expedite change. Having the right mindset helps. The people most successful at change are the people who let go quickly, once they realise they can't hold back the inevitable tide. They've learned to equate change with opportunity.

part four: the synergy

- *Neutral Zone — as we let go, we enter this second transition*

This is the 'grey area', uncomfortable to most of us. We use the Neutral Zone as an opportunity to take stock of our life and our priorities.

- *New Beginnings — finally, we accept that new beginnings are the next step*

The transitions are then complete (until we start the cycle again, with something else).

Ride the whirlpool

Here's a way of thinking that might help you next time you realise you're back in that state of being overwhelmed. Imagine you're a twig or a leaf, caught in a whirlpool. You're spinning near the centre of this vortex. At first it seems that you're way out of control, but in fact the movement of the water will eventually cast you out to the side of the pond. Even if the water overwhelms you for a brief moment, you're light enough to rise again to the surface; very soon the current will push you into the quieter waters, the new situation.

As a piece of human driftwood, thrown around by the twists and turns of fate, you've got two choices: fight against the current, or flow with it. As you learn to recognise the sensation of spinning too fast, you'll also learn to welcome the sensation, to relax, even in a state of seeming confusion. It's a great sign that the quiet water, the solution, the change, is very close. So, enjoy the ride and don't stress — it will be easier soon.

Change is neither good nor bad, but thinking makes it so. And we can't stop change, so let's learn to manage the thinking!

2: Pitfalls to avoid

Don't believe that yesterday's solutions will solve today's

problems. For instance, technology and globalisation are reshaping the way we get the word out about our business and services. Compare advertising before and after the Internet. Instead of wasting time looking back, or refusing to embrace technology, focus on the 'what' and 'how' of your solutions.

Don't assume that present trends will continue. To stay ahead, trend watch and be ready to alter direction in response to change. Mark Twain said, 'It isn't what we don't know that hurts us, it's what we think we know, that isn't true.' Don't neglect the opportunities offered by future change. In every change something is lost and something gained. Be first to spot the advantage in change before the window of opportunity closes.

3: New skills: 16 strategies to deal with change

(Some of these points have been expanded in other sections of the book.)

1. Use these five 'Choice of Behaviour' questions to clear your thinking:

    Why are we making this change?
    When is this change going to occur?
    How are we going to do it?
    What's in it for others?
    Who will be affected?

2. Speed up. Slow response kills companies and careers. Delete unnecessary steps and procedures.

3. Be a fast decision-maker. 'He who hesitates is lost' was never truer than now. Seek out accurate information, apply it to the best of your ability, and get on with the job. (More on decision-making in Chapter 16.)

4. Reshape your job: constantly realign your work as your organisation reshapes itself to survive.

part four: the synergy

5 Be 100 percent responsible for yourself: manage your career, growth, job, morale … none of us is safe from change. Learn new skills, go the extra mile, and be prepared for new roles and opportunities.

6 Define the givens, controllables, and the negotiables in the situation, and don't waste time beating your head against a brick wall. Apply the Alcoholics Anonymous prayer. 'God, grant me the serenity to accept the things I cannot change, courage to change the things I can, and the wisdom to know the difference.'

7 Add value: contribute more than you cost. Think contribution, not static longevity. What suggestions for improvement can you come up with? What processes have you noticed that are not efficient? What equipment needs fixing or replacing? And what can you personally contribute, rather than saying, 'The company should do something.'

8 Sharpen your customer-service skills: anticipate where the customers' needs will be, before they get there. When we go through change, it's easy to overlook details that impact on customer satisfaction. Stay in close touch with your customers; ask their opinions.

9 Find your rock, your safe place, where you can retreat from the world and recharge. Perhaps it's out in the wild, galloping your horse along a beach, a fast ride on a motorbike, a day in the garden, coffee with friends. For a guy it may be his garage or shed. What about giving yourself a duvet day, eiderdown day, doona day, mental health day (the labels vary from country to country) — a delicious and luxurious day in bed, reading, resting by yourself — or not, as your choice may be!

into the future

10 Be a stress buster: spot warning signs of impending burnout. Learn to set clear demarcations between the parts of your life to save you from burnout. Someone working at non-stop full stretch is riding for a fall — we're not machines, and even machines stop for regular maintenance! For instance, block out email-free days, schedule in holidays at the beginning of the year, have a three-day weekend every six weeks or two months. All these strategies and more keep the stress levels and exhaustion at a manageable level. Watch that your staff don't keep working at break-neck speed. No matter how efficient it seems to be in the short term, those who don't include daily recharge breaks become less and less effective.

11 Recuperation needs to happen every day. The body works in a series of circadian cycles. One of them is the Ultradian Rhythm. Our 'up' cycle lasts 90–120 minutes, and then we dip into a 20-minute rest and recuperation cycle. If we don't take regular breaks our system has no chance to rebuild. Athletes know this, hence their rests between hard bursts of activity. The same principle applies for 'corporate athletes'. (For more on this topic, check out Lesley Gillett's *Sleep Your Way to Success* and *The Power of Full Engagement* by Jim Loehr and Tony Schwartz.)

12 Learn to say no politely but appropriately. It's one of the most successful time-management tools! Know your top three priorities at work and at home. This gives you an anchor for decisions. If you're not good at it, practise on small things until you learn. Too many managers think they 'have to be there for their people'. However, when their marriage has disintegrated, or they've dropped dead from overwork, the company will still be there (unless it's their

part four: the synergy

own, in which case they drastically jeopardise the welfare of their staff by acting as if they're indispensable).

13 Precisely communicate goals, roles and expectations to staff, as discussed in earlier chapters. They need to keep abreast of the changes. If people in your company are stressed, your company is at risk. We're only as strong as our weakest link; when we feel out of control we're at our most vulnerable.

14 Think strategically in all things: monitor change inside and outside the industry. Get fast access to information, but don't worry if you haven't read today's headlines — someone will tell you if anything earth-shattering has happened.

15 Become excellent at environmental scanning, at seeking for new trends, new patterns. What's changing? Look for the signs; there are opportunities in emerging trends. For instance, a records-management company realised that as more and more information became electronically transmitted they risked jeopardising their profitable business unless they also offered support for electronic archival management.

16 Sharpen your focus constantly. Don't forget to step outside your traditional arena — it sharpens your creative thinking. Network outside your industry, skim non-traditional media, listen to your kids, become a people- and trend-watcher. Notice what's happening among the innovators of society; if you can learn to notice repeated patterns there, you're quite likely looking at a future trend. Malcolm Gladwell, in his excellent little book *The Tipping Point*, describes how Lambesis, a small PR company, used information gleaned from trend-watching to help turn the specialist Airwalk skateboard shoes into a huge mass market hit.

(Inspired by Leon Martel, *Mastering Change, the Key to Business Success*.)

into the future

Information overwhelm

An external sign of stress, which sometimes equals 'change occurring', is huge piles of information waiting to be looked at. How big is your pile? Are there magazines you subscribe to and don't read? Newsletters you receive, either by mail or email, that wait ever more sadly for you to notice them? Do you suffer guilt and mental stress fractures each time you look at these pregnantly bountiful piles?

It's time to recognise that information is not wisdom. We're surrounded by more information than anyone can handle. People will be paid in the future not for *knowing* much, but for our ability to *filter out* much. Learn to block the mind traffic, the overload of information, identify quickly what's relevant, and transmute that knowledge to applicable wisdom.

Think of your mind as a funnel. Into that funnel information tries to flood. We're surrounded by millions of disparate pieces of information all day long. As we filter that information to cut out the garbage, what's left (if we do it right) is knowledge.

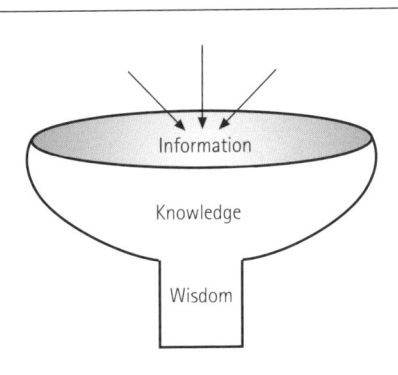

Figure 24 • The wisdom funnel

part four: the synergy

Some will be useful; much will be interesting but of no particular use right now. It's still too much to handle.

From knowledge we need to filter again, to distil right down to the essence, to the guts of the matters we *need* to know about. This becomes wisdom we can use and apply.

Effective dynamic change requires the four stages of team development

Let's finish this chapter on change with team development; how we nurture our teams to grow into future leaders; how we shift from managing the work to managing the workplace; how to create an environment where people can contribute to their potential.

Some of you may say, 'Why grow new leaders? Doesn't that put my job at risk? What if someone becomes as good as me?' One of the most important roles of leadership is to make yourself redundant. If you're not growing at least as fast as your team, you're not stretching yourself in readiness for new opportunities. A leader who's indispensable is a threat to the organisation. Life is full of uncertainty; we never know when something will happen to us, and if we're the only one who can do a job, we put our organisation under serious threat. The first thing a good leader does is begin to groom a successor.

To become powerful, you must give power away. Some managers seem to believe that to 'give power' means 'let the team loose' on a project, and that if they've passed the task over, they have to take the consequences of the team's efforts. Naturally enough, that's a scary thought for a responsible leader! What if they get it wrong! If a group hasn't had enough training, direction and experience, or they haven't grasped a solid overview of other strategic issues facing the company, of course they'll make decisions based on the limited data they've been given. And then they're more than likely to produce flawed results. The outcome can only be frustration on all parts. Instead, team development is a dynamic evolutionary process in which all parties are involved.

In Chapter 16 we discussed the four stages to effective delegation: directing, coaching, supporting and delegating. This related to training an individual. There is a series of similar steps to effective development of a team.

Step 1: Educate
Although managers make decisions and direct their team's activities, they explain issues to them, tell them about the decisions they made, and why they made those choices. A surprising number of managers make decisions and don't share the thinking — instead they share just enough to get the outcome. When you tell people what's going on, they're being prepared for higher-level involvement; they're learning by osmosis, even when they don't realise it.

Step 2: Ask for input
The manager asks the team for suggestions, applies their suggestions where possible, and keeps the team informed at all stages. If their recommendations can't be applied, they're told why.

Step 3: Involve fully
Discuss and work together collaboratively. The manager and well-informed team discuss all aspects of the situation, in full, and decisions are made collectively. A well-run voluntary organisation, based on sound democratic principles, generally works like this. Consensus on key issues is gained before the group acts. They share responsibility, accountability and risk taking.

part four: the synergy

Step 4: Transfer responsibility

The manager delegates the decision-making to the team, or individuals within the team, who operate autonomously. They tell the manager what they've done, as relevant, and take full responsibility for the outcomes.

If leaders don't understand these steps, or haven't communicated the level of responsibility they've given to a team, they lay themselves wide open for frustration and disempowerment of their people.

> *Abby was the new chair of her local parent-teacher association. She'd seen the previous chair run himself into the ground because of poor delegation skills, so decided to actively involve as many of her executive committee as possible. Subcommittees were established for all the core tasks, a leader was appointed for each subcommittee, and they were encouraged to seek assistants from the parents who weren't on the elected team. Abby felt that this would be a good way to involve more of the less active parents in the running of the school affairs, and her team enthusiastically supported the idea.*
>
> *Brendan, one of the long-standing members, took on responsibility for fundraising. He gathered around him a small subcommittee just as Abby had suggested, and started running his own monthly meetings. All manner of complex and time-consuming money-making suggestions flowed forth to the main executive — too many for them to handle. Because Brendan's focus went into the fundraising, his own area of interest, he didn't always get to the main meetings. Therefore he didn't fully understand that the executive had inherited a number of serious issues, including a disciplinary matter with one of the school staff. To the rest of the executives, and to Abby, major fundraising events, although important, didn't hit the top of their radar screen right then.*

into the future

A few months into her term, Abby was surprised to receive a very curt request from Brendan to attend one of his subcommittee meetings. To her surprise she found that he and his team felt unsupported, unheard, unappreciated and frustrated.

As well as Brendan's low awareness of the other issues the executive were dealing with, a couple of other communication factors muddied the waters.

He didn't send his reports through until the night before the main executive meetings, which were always held in the morning. This meant that Abby had no time to consider the recommendations, or circulate them to the rest of the executive, until after their meeting.

Neither he nor Abby talked together very much; because they were both busy their main dialogue was by email.

Had she known more about the process of team development, she would have realised she wanted them to work at a Step 2 level. However, they interpreted their mandate as being somewhere between Steps 3 and 4. Both sides were responsible for communication breakdowns, neither understood the development cycle, and they had to work three times as hard to repair the situation.

Figure 25 • The development cycle

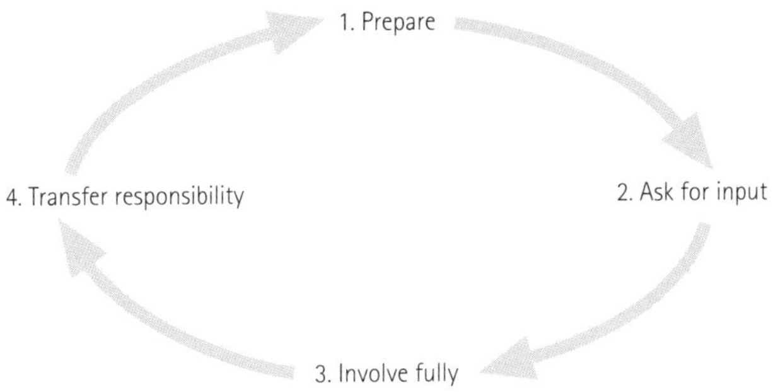

1. Prepare
2. Ask for input
3. Involve fully
4. Transfer responsibility

One last point about well-developed teams: they're more productive. An employee who doesn't feel very important won't worry about the little time wasters that cuddle in for comfort. However, if they feel that they 'own' their job they'll be much harder on their own time inefficiencies. Given the opportunity to take responsibility, they'll work to their maximum instead of working to rule.

Have fun managing change, information and your powerful team. It's a work of art and a gift to those around you. As Canadian poet Bliss Carman said, 'Set me a task in which I can put something of myself and it is a task no longer; it is a joy, it is an art.'

Leadership lessons

- Leaders can only help their team manage change if they know how to manage their own changes.

- To manage change, we must understand the process of what's happening, identify the pitfalls and apply new skills.

- Four stages of change — denial, resistance, exploration and commitment.

- Three stages of transition — letting go, the neutral zone and new beginnings.

- Ride the whirlpool; enjoy the ride. The quiet waters wait.

- Change is neither good nor bad — it's thinking makes it so.

- Pitfalls:
  Don't believe that yesterday's solutions will solve today's problems.

into the future

Don't assume that present trends will continue.

Don't neglect the opportunities offered by future change.

☑ 16 strategies to deal with change:
Use the five 'Choice of Behaviour' questions to clear your thinking.
Speed up.
Be a fast decision-maker.
Reshape your job.
Be 100 percent responsible for yourself.
Don't waste time beating your head against a brick wall.
Add value.
Anticipate the customers' needs.
Find your safe place, regularly retreat from the world, and recharge.
Be a stress buster.
Recuperation needs to happen every day.
Learn to say no.
Precisely communicate goals, roles and expectations to your people.
Think strategically in all things.
Become excellent at environmental scanning.
Constantly sharpen your focus.

☑ Information is not wisdom.

☑ People will be paid in the future not for *knowing* much, but for our ability to *filter out* much.

☑ To become powerful, you must give power away.

☑ The four stages of team development: educate; ask for input; involve fully; transfer responsibility.

summary of part four

15 What are my team's wants, needs and strengths?

☆ The only way I can get you to do anything is by giving you what you want.' — Dale Carnegie.

☆ Use profiling tools to get the right staff — empathy and liking will tend to get you someone like yourself.

☆ Hire in a hurry and repent at leisure.

☆ Understand what makes your people tick and you'll get the results you want, instead of running perpetual damage control.

☆ Maslow's Hierarchy of Needs shows us five levels of need. A need is a motivator: once it is satisfied it no longer motivates.

☆ Different generations are motivated by different things.

16 How do I get the best out of them?

☆ If you want to lead, get into the trenches.

☆ A great leader provides focus and clarity.

summary of part four

☆ Good leaders are fast decision-makers.

☆ Practise lateral (or creative) thinking.

☆ Become an excellent manager of your time choices.

☆ Run effective meetings — short, sharp, focused and to the point.

☆ Good delegators increase their own power by sharing it with others.

☆ Delegation is a four-stage train ride, not a one-step destination.

☆ Look for ways to make yourself redundant.

☆ Don't put focus on what's wrong; praise to the goal.

17 Into the future — leaders who can lead through change

☆ Leaders can only help their team manage change if they know how to manage their own changes.

☆ To manage change, we must understand the process of what's happening, identify the pitfalls and apply new skills.

☆ Four stages of change — denial, resistance, exploration and commitment.

☆ Three stages of transition — letting go, the neutral zone and new beginnings.

☆ Ride the whirlpool; enjoy the ride. The quiet waters wait.

☆ Change is neither good nor bad — it's thinking makes it so.

part four: the synergy

☆ Pitfalls:
   Don't believe that yesterday's solutions will solve today's problems.
   Don't assume that present trends will continue.
   Don't neglect the opportunities offered by future change.

☆ Apply some of the 16 change strategies and you'll cope far better.

☆ Information is not wisdom.

☆ People will be paid in the future not for *knowing* much, but for our ability to *filter out* much.

☆ To become powerful, you must give power away.

☆ The four stages of team development: educate; ask for input; involve fully; transfer responsibility.

last words

We've covered the highways and byways of practical, common-sense leadership. You'll have refreshed some knowledge, expanded your thinking with new ideas, and been reminded of stories good and bad in your own experience, by reading the true-life stories we've shared. (Many names, industries and locations have been changed to protect the identities of the examples, but we're proud to have shared the stories of two of our 'shining star' past employers, Wilma Snow and Phil Molloy.)

We trust that in this practical leadership guide you found concepts and strategies to help your journey as a leader/employer, and that you enjoy integrating the ideas into your daily practice as an employer of choice.

As you progress through your journey of leadership, may you:

- ☆ feel confident in living your purpose, values and vision.
- ☆ become a powerful, effective leader and a strategic thinker.
- ☆ enjoy a wonderful working climate, with such powerful synergy operating in your workplace that your team grows from strength to strength.
- ☆ have people lining up with eagerness to work with you, as Jim Goodnight did.

Enjoy the journey, and we'll see you down the road.

appendix 1 • strategic planning template

Step 1 Pre-planning. Choose the facilitator Set timeline and logistics Select the planning team	
Where are we now?	
Step 2 Mission. Why do we exist? What are our services?	
Step 3 Vision. What's our aim? What will we be in the future? How will we look to others?	
Step 4 Values. What do we stand for – what are our beliefs, ethics and standards?	
Step 5 Assess the previous strategic plan and current goals. What can we learn from what we've already done? Are our current goals still relevant?	

© Robyn Pearce and LaVonn Steiner, *Getting a Grip on Leadership* (Reed, 2004). May be photocopied for non-commercial use.

Where should we be going?

Step 6 Scanning – external.
What are the top five opportunities and threats we should consider?

Step 7 Scanning – internal.
What are the top five strengths and weaknesses we should consider?

Step 8 Critical issues.
What are our four most urgent, most important issues?

How should we get there?

Step 9 Key goal areas.
What are the four most important areas we must achieve in?

Step 10 Objectives, Action Plans and Timelines.
What specific measurable steps must we take and what deadlines do we need to reach our goals?

Step 11 Measures.
What targets will indicate our progress (they may be numerical)?

Step 12 Final Review and Evaluation.
Have we covered everything? Date? Timelines? Written down? Who? How often? How tracked? Rewards? Indicators?

© Robyn Pearce and LaVonn Steiner, *Getting a Grip on Leadership* (Reed, 2004). May be photocopied for non-commercial use.

appendix 2 • the results calendar — Gantt chart

Legend: In process ⟶ Target Completion Date ⊙

Year:

Outcomes to Track	JAN	FEB	MAR	APR	MAY	JUN	JUL	AUG	SEP	OCT	NOV	DEC	✓

© Robyn Pearce and LaVonn Steiner, *Getting a Grip on Leadership* (Reed, 2004). May be photocopied for non-commercial use.

appendix 2a • the results calendar — Gantt chart (example)

Legend: In process ➔   Target Completion Date ⊙

Goal: *Administration. The new XYZ small business will establish basic business systems.*

Year: 1

Outcomes to Track	JAN	FEB	MAR	APR	MAY	JUN	JUL	AUG	SEP	OCT	NOV	DEC	
Objective 1.1: By 30 April (year 1) the marketing manager will expedite a three-year marketing plan.	➔	➔	➔	⊙									✓
Objective 1.2: By 30 June (year 1) the XYZ business office will implement an effective performance appraisal system.				➔	➔	⊙							✓
Objective 1.3: By 30 September (year 1) the training and development manager will establish an orientation for collaborating partners.							➔	➔	⊙				✓

Year: 2

Objective 1.4: By 31 December (year 2) the business manager will complete the upgrade of technology equipment.					➔	➔	➔	➔	➔	➔	➔	⊙	

Continue planning goals and objectives for each year of the strategic plan

© Robyn Pearce and LaVonn Steiner, *Getting a Grip on Leadership* (Reed, 2004). May be photocopied for non-commercial use.

appendix 3 • action work plan

Strategic Priority

State the strategic goal

My Goal

Item(s) you have taken responsibility for

Name/Position

You are responsible for this priority whether the action steps are delegated or not

Resources

List all those resources available to you, for example outside consultants, other managers, books, tapes and so on.

List all the specific action steps that must be implemented to accomplish objectives. All steps, no matter how small they seem, should be documented with person responsible and completion date.

Ensure person named fully understands and is fully committed to the action step, knows how it affects other steps, and consequence of non-completion by deadline.

For any costs that need recording.

ACTION STEPS	WHO	START	COMPLETE	COST $

© Robyn Pearce and LaVonn Steiner, *Getting a Grip on Leadership* (Reed, 2004). May be photocopied for non-commercial use.

appendix 3a • action work plan (example)

State the strategic goal	**Strategic Priority**	Implement an effective performance appraisal system no later than 30 June (year)
Item(s) you have taken responsibility for	**My Goal**	Develop and implement consistent job descriptions for all positions no later than 30 June (year)
You are responsible for this priority whether the action steps are delegated or not	**Name/Position**	Jane Smith, Assistant Human Resource Director
List all those resources available to you, for example outside consultants, other managers, books, tapes and so on.	**Resources**	Job Descriptions Handbook; Personnel Department, Mary Jones

List all the specific action steps that must be implemented to accomplish objectives. All steps, no matter how small they seem, should be documented with person responsible and completion date.

Ensure person named fully understands and is fully committed to the action step, knows how it affects other steps, and consequence of non-completion by deadline.

For any costs that need recording.

ACTION STEPS	WHO	START	COMPLETE	COST $
1. Define the essential ingredients and format to a legal, effective job description	Kathleen Schlosser	1 March	28 April	
2. Put in place a committee for job description review	Lori Shereck	15 March	14 May	
3. Set up controls that assign each manager to rewrite job descriptions according to requirements	Madonna Stanford	15 April	17 May	
4. Hold training sessions for managers on job descriptions, and communicate the requirements and format	Don Boehm, Cyndy Gaj	19 May	20 May	Est. $4500
5. Have managers evaluate existing job descriptions, rewrite and submit to committee	Kathleen Schlosser, All managers	1 April	4 June	
6. Have committee review and give approval of each job description	Committee	1 June	20 June	
7. Set up control systems for re-evaluations of existing and new job descriptions	Madonna Stanford	15 May	25 June	

© Robyn Pearce and LaVonn Steiner, *Getting a Grip on Leadership* (Reed, 2004). May be photocopied for non-commercial use.

resources

Chapter 10: Communication is king!
Who Killed the Sale? First produced in 1991, remade 2000. Available from International Tele-Film, http://www.itf.ca.

Chapter 11: How the leader impacts the climate
Les Giblin's *How to Have Power and Confidence in Dealing With People* — Robyn's favourite on the magic of great relationships.

Ingrid Bacci's *The Art of Effortless Living* — an excellent book on this and other aspects of relationships, as well as living effortlessly.

Blaine Lee's *The Power Principle* — LaVonn's recommendation for how to influence with honour.

Ronald B. Adler's *Communicating at Work* — a straightforward read on principles and practices for business and the professions.

Sam Horn's *What's Holding You Back* — an excellent book for self-development, full of questions and self-assessments.

Chapter 15: What are my team's wants, needs and strengths?
Staff Selection Tool. Target Training International, www.ttidisc.com. Available in New Zealand from Extra Dimensions NZ Ltd, phone + 64-9-376 1603, www.ednz.co.nz.

What Makes People Tick? Profiling Questionnaire, plus other resources. Developed by and available from Des Hunt, Personal & Professional Growth Concepts Pty Ltd, phone +61-8-8269 5970.

Enneagram: http://www.enneagraminstitute.com/ennegram.asp.

Herman: http://www.hbdi.com.

Kolbe: http://www.Kolbe.com.

Littauer: http://www.classervices.com/FlorenceLittauer.html.

Myers Briggs: do a Google search for your nearest supplier.

Wilson Learning Styles: http://www.wilsonlearning.com.

bibliography

Adler, Ronald B. *Communicating at Work*. Random House, New York, 1983, third edition 1989.

Bacci, Ingrid. *The Art of Effortless Living*. Bantam, New York, 2002.

Biggs, Susan, and Horgan, Kerry Fallon. *Time on, Time out! Flexible Work Solutions to Keep Your Life in Balance*. Allen & Unwin, Australia, 1998.

Blanchard, Kenneth. *Leadership and the One Minute Manager*. Fontana/ Collins, London, 1987.

Brantley, John T. *Performance Coaching — Skills Based Strategies for Developing Self-propelled People*. Benson & Latimer Press, Georgia, 2001.

Bridges, William. *Transitions — Making Sense of Life's Changes*. Nicholas Brealey, London, 1996.

Buzan, Tony. *Make the Most of Your Mind*. Colt Books, Cambridge, 1977. Pan, London, 1981. (There are many other titles by Tony Buzan.)

Byham, William C., and Cox, Jeff. *Zapp! The Lightning of Empowerment. How to Improve Productivity, Quality, and Employee Satisfaction*. Ballantine, New York, 1988.

Cairnes, Margot. *Approaching the Corporate Heart*. Simon & Schuster, Australia, 1998.

Canfield, Jack; Hansen, Mark Victor; Rogerson, Maida; Rutte, Martin; and Clauss, Tim. *Chicken Soup for the Soul at Work — 101 Stories of Courage, Compassion and Creativity in the Workplace*. Health Communications, Florida, 1996. (Includes a story by LaVonn Steiner.)

Carnegie, Dale. *How to Win Friends and Influence People*. Simon & Schuster, New York, 1981. Vermilion, London, revised edition 1998.

Coopersmith, Stanley. *Antecedents of Self Esteem*. Consulting

bibliography

Coopersmith, Stanley. *Antecedents of Self Esteem*. Consulting Psychologists Press, California, second edition 1981.

Credit Union Magazine. Complete Staff Incentives Survey 1998. Credit Union National Association, Washington DC.

De Bono, Edward. *Six Thinking Hats*. Viking, Harmondsworth, 1986. Revised edition Little, Brown, Boston, Massachusetts, 1999.

Dudley, George W., and Goodson, Shannon L. *The Psychology of Sales Call Reluctance, Earning What You're Worth in Sales*. Behavioral Sciences Research Press, Dallas, Texas, 1999.

Futurist, The. March/April 2000. 'Know the difference between the four generations — work from wants.'

Gardner, Howard. *Frames of Mind: The Theory of Multiple Intelligences*. Basic, New York, 1983.

Giblin, Les. *How to Have Confidence and Power in Dealing with People*. Prentice Hall, New York, 1956, reprinted 1986, 1999.

Gillett, Lesley. *Sleep Your Way to Success*. Time Out Seminar Company, Australia, 2000. http://www.tosc.com.au/

Gladwell, Malcolm. *The Tipping Point: How Little Things Can Make a Big Difference*. Time Warner, New York, 2000, sixth reprint 2003.

Goleman, Daniel. *Working with Emotional Intelligence*. Bloomsbury, London, 1999.

Hall, Michael, and Bodenhamer, Bob. *Figuring out People: Design Engineering with Meta-programs. Deepening Understanding of People for Better Rapport, Relationships and Influence*. Anglo American Book Company, Wales, 1997.

Harris, Thomas. *I'm OK, You're OK*. Avon, New York, 1969.

Horn, Sam. *What's Holding You Back?* St Martin's Giffin, New York, 1997.

Hunt, Des. *What Makes People Tick?* McGraw-Hill, Australia, 1988, reprinted 1991.

———. *How to Sell the Way Your Customer Buys and Close the Sale Every Time*. Personal and Professional Growth Concepts, Australia, 1998.

Kouzes, James, and Posner, Barry. *The Leadership Challenge*. Jossey-Bass, San Francisco, third edition 2002.

Kubler-Ross, Elisabeth. *On Death and Dying*. Touchstone, New York, 1969, reprinted 1997.

Lamont, Georgeanne. *The Spirited Business — Success Stories of Soul-Friendly Companies*. Hodder & Stoughton, London, 2002.

Lee, Blaine. *The Power Principle*. Simon & Schuster, New York, 1997.

Loehr, Jim, and Schwartz, Tony. *The Power of Full Engagement*. Allen & Unwin, Australia, 2003.

Martel, Leon. *Mastering Change, the Key to Business Success*. Simon & Schuster, New York, 1986.

Millman, Dan. *Way of the Peaceful Warrior*. H.J. Kramer, California, 1980, reprinted 1984, 2000.

Moore, Christopher W. *The Mediation Process*. Jossey-Bass, San Francisco, 1996.

Moore, Lt Gen. Harold G, and Galloway, Joseph L. *We Were Soldiers Once ... and Young*. Random, New York, 1992, reprinted 2002.

Orwell, George. 'Politics and the English language.' An essay, 1946. http://www.resort.com/~prime8/Orwell/patee.html

Pastor, Joan. 'Empowerment: what it is and what it is not'. From *Empowerment in Organizations*, Vol. 4, No. 2, 1996: 5–7. www.jpa-international.com

Price, Carol. *How to Present a Professional Image*. Tape series, © 1999. http://www.carolprice.com/books_videos.htm

Seitel, Fraser P. *The Practice of Public Relations*. Prentice Hall, New York, 2000, eighth edition.

Semler, Ricardo. *Maverick*. Arrow, London, 1994.

Taylor, Stephen. *The Employee Retention Handbook*. Chartered Institute of Personnel and Development, London, 2002.

Yates, Mick. Website and ezine: http://www.leader-values.com

Yew Kam Keong. *You Are Creative — Let Your Creativity Bloom*. Mindbloom, Kuala Lumpur, 1998, second edition 2002. http://www.mindbloom.net/

about the authors

LaVonn Steiner MS, CM

LaVonn Steiner improves performance and productivity through leadership coaching.

She has delivered over 1100 motivational presentations to leaders from 29 countries and four continents. She holds two masters degrees, is a certified manager, a trained scientist, and has been a healthcare manager for 20 years. Before launching EXCEL LEADERSHIP Inc, a consulting and coaching enterprise, she directed a medical teaching programme that ranked third out of 400 similar programmes in the US.

She is a product of her own teachings, from her humble beginnings as an on-the-job-trained healthcare employee to a nationally awarded healthcare manager. LaVonn was honoured in Washington DC as National Educator of the Year for coaching and mentoring. She has a record second to none when it comes to achieving results and coaching individuals.

LaVonn is a featured author of the number-one *New York Times* best-selling book series *Chicken Soup for the Soul at Work.*

She developed this leadership system as a healthcare manager and now spreads her message worldwide in coaching, speeches and seminars through her company. Client businesses include the Mayo Clinic, Dupont, the American Institute of Banks, Rosenbluth International, State Farm Insurance Companies, and many government agencies.

Robyn Pearce CSP

As this book was written, Robyn was serving as President of the National Speakers Association of New Zealand. During her term the membership grew by 80 percent, many improvements were integrated, finances dramatically improved, major sponsorship was secured,

about the authors

and a team approach involved more members than previously in running the association.

At a business level, from 1992 she has run an international training and speaking business in the South Pacific, working with associates and contractors, managing staff and working with senior managers to improve the productivity and effectiveness of their companies. Her clients include many major corporates around Australia and New Zealand, such as LJ Hooker (Australia), Lendlease, Fuji Xerox, Sanitarium, Bayleys Real Estate, Vodafone, many educational groups, and government and state departments such as Landcare (NZ), Road Transport Authority NSW (RTA), and NSW Heritage Office.

Apart from business experience, many of Robyn's lessons have come from involvement in community and professional associations, as well as raising six children. After serving on many committees and taking leadership roles at both local and national levels, she's found many parallels between association, corporate, non-profit and family leadership needs.

Other titles by Robyn Pearce

Getting a Grip on Time. Reed Publishing (NZ) Ltd, 1996, fifth reprint 2003.

About Time — 120 Tips for Those with No Time. Reed Publishing (NZ) Ltd, 2001, reprinted 2003.

Getting a Grip on Life — Goals Toolkit. Co-authored with Trish Flower. Getting A Grip Publishing, Auckland, NZ, 2003. Available from http://www.gettingagriponlife.com.

Getting a Grip on the Paper War — Managing Information in the Modern Office. Reed Publishing (NZ) Ltd, 2003.

index

analytical thinking 71
appraisals and performance
  reviews 166
  rules 168
attraction
  law of 108
Blanchard, Kenneth, *Leadership and the One Minute Manager* 239
career choices 47
change 244
  four stages of 246–47
  new skills 249
  process of 246
communication 114, 119, 125, 196
  chart 45
  checklist 131
  competencies 45
  science of 119
  styles 116
  three Es of effective communication 121
  Who Killed the Sale? 120
conflict 171, 172, 199, 200
  complaints 171, 200
  resolution 179
  steps to resolve 174
  unethical people checklist 181
  why it occurs 175
congruence 19, 20

critical issues 65, 76
De Bono, Edward 230
decision-making 226
  tips to improve 227
delegation 237
  four stages of 238
  reverse delegation 241
  tips 239
DISC profiling tool 208
Drucker, Peter, *Harvard Law Review* 124
email 91, 184, 186
  writing tips 192
employee retention handbook 135
employee satisfaction audit 155
environment
  climate 91–94, 99, 197
  culture 90
  effective employees 98
  keys to leader impact 133
evaluation 65
expectation, law of 107
feedback 127, 159, 198
  essential steps 160
focus and clarity 225
foundation
  blocks 12, 52
  purpose 13
  strengths 44
  values 19

index

Franklin Close technique   228
Gantt chart   78, 266–69
gender differences   109
generational needs, wants and motivators   218
goals   76, 225
  action plans   77
  conflict   175
  objectives   77
  strategic   65
  time frames   77
  timelines   77
Goodnight, Jim, SAS   134
group decision-making style   229
Harris, Thomas, *You're OK, I'm OK*   116
Hierarchy of Needs   216–18
Hunt, Des   211
  What makes people tick?   213–14
intelligence   150
  emotional   150
  spiritual   151
internal tapes   103
lateral thinking techniques   230
leadership
  lessons   18, 24, 32, 43, 51, 67, 81, 85, 112, 132, 157, 169, 182, 194, 222, 243, 258
  measures   65
  principles   137–41
  self-knowledge   56
  systems   10
life balance   84, 110

listening
  effective   125
  feedback   127
  levels   126
  productive listening habits   130
  secrets   129
Maslow, Abraham   216
  Hierarchy of Needs   218
meetings
  agenda   236
  chairperson's role   234
  effective   233
  filtering questions   237
  process   234
  tips   235
mental well-being   106
mission statement   64, 70, 122
  example   17
  individual   16
  organisational   17
multiple management   146
NLP   143
objectives   65
peer recognition programmes   106
personnel selection   207
  DISC profiling tool   208
  interview questions   209
PESTS analysis   72
planning
  big picture   57
  blueprint for   69, 87
  definitions   64
  evaluation of   80

index

key elements of 63
life 84
strategic 56, 59–65, 68–69, 82, 86–87
team 66
traditional 59, 86
power 33
balance of 39
energy bubble 40
mental tapes 35
of the mind 42, 102
personal 13
place of 53
purpose 13
rules of 33
sources 36, 111
'red' time 231
respect 20
role models and influencers 25, 28
scanning 64
self-esteem 100
checklist 101
staff selection 207
DISC profiling tool 208
strengths
personal 44–45
success 26
filters to define 27
SWOT analysis 64, 71
external scanning 71
internal scanning 74
synergy 10, 204
team development 124, 254
development cycle 257
four stages of 255–57
time management tips 231
transactional analysis 116
Ultradian Rhythm 251
values 19, 71
core 20, 23, 64, 122
examples 23
lived 20
vision 55, 64, 70, 122, 225
wisdom funnel 253